"The Mindful Hiker o[...] r
plane of reflection an[...] d
be savored slowly pag[...]"

CAROL ADRIENNE, [...]
Author of *When Life Changes, Or You Wish it Would*

"The Mindful Hiker is an eloquent and important book for all concerned with coming into a deeper relationship with nature. Reading it will certainly open the door to self-discovery, heightened awareness of the environment, and enlightened action."

PETER BARNES, Director of Tomales Bay Institute
Author of *Who Owns the Sky? Our Common Assets and the Future of Capitalism*

"A fierce and aching spirit blows through this book – aching for freedom and joy, and from a heart bursting with love for the beauty and mystery of the natural world. Stephen Altschuler invites us to exault, rant, whine and fall in love with the great silence together with him. His words not only evoke the spirit of wild and free places but also provide inklings for us of ways to enter into and embody that same wisdom and freedom in our own hearts. This book is truly written as a gift from the heart – indeed, perhaps a more appropriate title would have been the 'The Heartful Hiker' – may every reader enjoy the journey through these pages and end up at home safely, wiser and more peaceful from the experience."

AMARO BHIKKHU
Abhayagiri Buddhist Monastery

"The Mindful Hiker reminds us of how Nature provides such a mirror of the beauty, majesty, and largesse found within the human spirit. Every path or trail provides the learning and opportunity that awaits us for increased solace, peace, and balance."

ANGELES ARRIEN, PH.D.
Cultural Anthropologist and author of *The Four-Fold Way* and *Sign of Life*

Enjoy!

Stephen Altschuler

Stephen Altschuler (signature)

The Mindful Hiker

On the Trail
to Find the Path

DeVorss Publications
Camarillo, California

The Mindful Hiker
Copyright ©2004 by Stephen Altschuler

All rights reserved. No part of this book may be reproduced or transmitted in any form or by any means, electronic or mechanical, including photocopying or recording, or by any information storage or retrieval system, except as may be expressly permitted by the 1976 Copyright Act or in writing by the Publisher.

ISBN: 0875167977
Library of Congress Control Number: 2003113782
FIRST EDITION, 2004

10 9 8 7 6 5 4 3 2 1

CIP information available upon request.

DeVorss & Company, Publisher
P.O. Box 1389
Camarillo CA 93011–1389
w w w . d e v o r s s . c o m

Printed in the United States of America

TABLE OF CONTENTS

For my Bubbe, Anna Odesky

ACKNOWLEDGMENTS

For their great teachings, guidance, and inspiration, a deep bow to Joshu Sasaki Roshi and Ajahn Sumedho.

For help and support in the writing and research of this book, thanks to Linda Allen, Peter Barnes and the Mesa Refuge, the staff of Point Reyes National Seashore, and naturalist Claire Peasley.

For their friendship and encouragement, thanks to Bob Bartel, Charlie Fisher, Terry Ojure, Barbara Renard, Mike Beckett, and Patrick Tribble.

Much thanks to my publisher and fellow hiker "on the trail to find the path," Gary Peattie; and to Monica Faulkner, as good an editor as any writer could hope for.

Thanks and much love to my mother, Rose, who, unfortunately passed away before she could be my most passionate book promoter. And to my father, Mo, who, if alive, wouldn't have given me much praise but would have kept the book on his nightstand.

Thanks to my family in Philadelphia, as well as my new family in Brazil, for their love and support.

And, of course, my deepest gratitude, affection, and love to my wife, Ruth, who mindfully and joyfully walks the trails with me.

Mountains cannot be surmounted
except by winding paths.

— Johann Wolfgang Von Goethe

The Mindful Hiker

Origins

Beginnings are like seedling roots—delicate, searching, resilient, as they become familiar with the surrounding soil. Mystery saturates beginnings, like the chicken or the egg, or our own birth. We barely remember our own beginnings, at least not consciously.

I recall the first time I walked Sky Trail, in July 1982, the way a very old man might remember the previous day: indistinctly, ambiguously, foggy about the exact details. The trail is located in the northern reaches of Point Reyes National Seashore, a moody, wild, light-filled hundred square miles of forest and sand and surf that spans the coast starting about 25 miles north of San Francisco.

I'd like to be able to recount a profound story about that event, to capture your attention with drama, insight, and serendipity, but, like many moments in life, it seemed only to be a nice place to walk that day.

Once, during a three-month meditation retreat, Buddhist teacher Jack Kornfield, one of the founders of Insight

1

Meditation Society in Barre, Massachusetts, commented, "Every moment is no more or less important than every other moment." At the time it was one of those revelations that snapped me to attention and appreciation of everything I was experiencing, from formal meditation on a cushion, to turning a doorknob and pulling open a door to get to another room, to tasting each bite of food at lunch. Whenever I reflect on that piece of wisdom, it reminds me to view each moment of life as a blessing, with such clarity and truth that its value and importance become crystal clear.

~

That first day on the trail was not a pretty one by California standards. July in the northern coastal part of the state often lives up to Mark Twain's remark about the coldest winter he'd ever spent being a summer in San Francisco. He was referring to the kind of fog that blows in off the always-chilly Pacific waters and hugs the ground for hours on end. The only ways to escape the cold dampness are to head inland a few miles, or to look for hikes above it. Given Sky Trail's billing as a gateway to the highest point in the park, I headed there with a good friend and favorite hiking companion, Bob Bartel, a carpenter and contractor whom I knew from back east and who had recently settled, as I had, in the Bay Area.

I first met Bob in 1977 at a Zen retreat in Massachusetts where he was living as a Zen student at the Cambridge Zen Center, under the tutelage of the Korean Zen Master Seung Sahn. I was down from New Hampshire, where I was living alone in a tiny cabin in the woods, for a taste of the big city, Zen style. It was my first Buddhist meditation retreat, and I had a tough time with the rigorous discipline and form. (I've detailed the entire experience in my previous book, *Sacred Paths and Muddy Places: Rediscovering Spirit in Nature.*) At the end of the seven-day retreat, Bob and I became fast friends, finding common ground in our spiritual practices and love of nature. Several years later, we met up again in northern California.

Our talks, unlike stereotypical male conversations about sports, work, and cars, ranged from relationships to the behavior of coyotes to spiritual practice, to philosophers and teachers like the Trappist philosopher-monk Thomas Merton, Sasaki Roshi, and the French philosopher and paleontologist Pierre Teilhard de Chardin. Bob eventually returned to his Christian contemplative roots and was practicing centering prayer with Father Thomas Keating, a Trappist who expanded upon Merton's work.

On that day, we started at the trailhead just off Limantour Road, the park's main artery, which nearly bisects its 100 square miles. The trail starts as a fire road wide enough for two saddled horses and two hikers to walk abreast. We ascended steadily as tall Douglas firs thickened around us and narrow spurs of the trail eventually forced us into single file. Plateaus broke the climb, but the trail felt like other California trails the first time I had tried them. They had all seemed steep, with long, often winding ascents then jarring descents. Unlike Eastern forests, where thick woods can block views for much of a hike, Western trails often lead quickly to hike-stopping vistas. The views were inspiring, but the relentless ascents exhausted me at first even though I was in decent physical shape.

We followed the narrow Horse and Z Ranch trails—fingerlings of the Sky—as they curved up to an expansive view of

Drake's Bay and the Point Reyes headlands to the west. We were on the spine of Inverness Ridge, the range of forested hills along and around the crest of the Point Reyes Peninsula that closely parallels the San Andreas Fault, which slides like a talus slope every so often and causes cities to fall. Sky Trail and its tentacles account for about six of the park's 147 miles of trails, which also include trails through coastal dunes, beaches, chaparral, and along estuaries. Sky Trail rolls along this ridge with almost equal gains and losses of elevation as it passes through open meadows and a Douglas fir forest. The trail and the forest around it are home to bobcats, cougars, deer, peregrine falcons, ospreys, jackrabbits, foxes, badgers, elk, and several species of hawks and owls, including the endangered spotted owl. Sky Trail, one of the wildest and highest trails in the park, eventually descends to the open ocean views of Coast Trail, one of the world's most spectacular wild coastal trails.

What I remember most about that first hike is emerging into the sun above the fog bank at the 1,407-foot summit of Mount Wittenberg, the highest point on the Point Reyes promontory. In Kathmandu, Wittenberg would be little more than a knoll, but in the coastal California range above the fog it was impressive.

We sat there, Bob and I, and talked the talk of the early 1980s—troublesome relationships, money woes, figuring out how to get a foothold in the roiling, creative, vibrant, and somewhat unsettling culture of California. Since coming back to the "real world" from my New Hampshire cabin, I'd been trying to piece together a livelihood using the master's degree in counseling that I'd picked up a few years before, but the California licensing board was notorious for giving a hard time to those

4

with out-of-state degrees, and I'd settled for a part-time job at a community college where I offered outreach music and exercise classes to nursing homes. I had also started an underground psychotherapy practice specializing in people who practiced meditation. I wasn't earning much, but I was sharing a house in Berkeley with my fiancée, Anita, who later became my second wife, and two other men, so my expenses were low.

The fog slowly receded and revealed more and more of Drake's Bay, Limantour Estero, the Point Reyes headlands, and the sea. From where we sat on the ridge, the ocean looked like a huge, living Monet canvas. If I were a skilled storyteller, I would have recalled my feelings around that first sighting of the ocean from Inverness Ridge, but our conversation muted the impact of the firsts on that hike. One quality of the trail that defined it as special, though, was already filtering through to me. Perhaps it was the roll of the landscape, punctuated with firs that stood like exclamation marks wanting to be noticed. Perhaps it was the density of the forest, with its wide margins of meadows and open views. Perhaps it was the fog, all-enveloping in the morning yet retreating at noon to reveal the edges of the sea and the play of the sun sparkling on the water. I think, though, that it was actually the trail's smell—that balm of fir and pine duff and the decay of fallen trees, the heavy dampness permeated by the salt sea air, the vitality of breezes far from car fumes.

As Bob and I talked that day, in the intervals between words and thoughts and laughter, the qualities of the place entered my soul, and my relationship with Sky Trail took root.

~

I was not fully conscious of those qualities on that first walk, but the trail's diversity, its contrasts of fog and sun, its muted shafts of light bending around and through the forest canopy, its wide and narrow places that made walking with a friend a dance in which we moved side by side and then word-lessly into single file as if we were reading each other's minds, its silence, were the first sketches for a painting of the trail that would eventually live in my soul.

Science could describe and explain much of what the trail is physically, but not its inherent unifying spirit. Everything on and around the trail is interrelated. The death of a grasshopper entangled in an orb web is life for the spider at the center of that tapestry. In a hundred years, an old grandfather fir, felled in a storm, will have turned to humus that adds to the rich growing medium of the forest floor. Modern science quantifies and sep-arates, creating boundaries to gain some sense of control over nature—fulfilling, in a subtle, backdoor way, the biblical decree that humanity shall have dominion over the natural world.

"The ultimate metaphysical secret," wrote philosopher Ken Wilber in *No Boundary*, "if we dare to state it so simply, is that there are no boundaries in the universe. Boundaries are illusions, prod-ucts not of reality but of the way we map and edit reality. And while it is fine to map out the territory, it is fatal to confuse the two." This is difficult for rational, linear-thinking, science-raised people to buy, for we feel more comfortable compartmentalizing the world. Fragment the world into its parts without attention to the sum of those parts, and the next move is often denigration, which we've seen time and again. The sum of the parts of this uni-verse includes the words God, Spirit, Love, and Higher Power and are likewise troublesome for science, which can't categorize and subdivide them the way it has tried to do with the parts of nature. "You can't put love into a test tube," scientists might say, "so we'll just discount it." (And isn't modern science essentially just so much counting, with engineering having picked up where original scientific theories left off?)

Poetry, which "should not mean but be," as Archibald MacLeish put it, comes closest to describing what science would likely fail to explain. Consider, for example, this poem by Wendell Berry:

THE PEACE OF WILD THINGS

When despair for the world grows in me
and I wake in the night at the least sound
in fear of what my life and my children's lives may be,
I go and lie down where the wood drake
rests in his beauty on the water, and the great heron feeds.
I come into the peace of wild things
who do not tax their lives with forethought
of grief. I come into the presence of still water.
And I feel above me the day-blind stars
waiting with their light. For a time
I rest in the grace of the world, and am free.

To try to explain or analyze this feeling is to destroy it. Love saturates the trail—that same love you see in your cat's eyes, or your dog's, or your python's, or your bird's, or your baby's. You know it when you feel it, even though you may not have words for it. This is why everything in the forest grows so profusely and recovers so quickly in the wake of fire or drought or flood or storm. Love and death grow the forest. They are inseparable.

EXPLORING YOUR PATH

> Take 10 minutes to think back to your first significant experience with nature. Perhaps it involved a tree outside your house, a nearby park, even a vacant lot across the street. Go back to this memory and try to recapture your impressions. How did you feel? Who was with you? What was happening in your life at the time? Take another few minutes to record some of these impressions in your journal.

> What does "peace of mind" mean to you? What are its specific dimensions –mental, physical, spiritual? If peace of mind were an object that you could hold, what color would it be? What texture would it have? What fragrance would it have? What sound would it make?

> Is there a poem in literature that describes the peace of being in a wild place? If you don't know of one, take a few minutes to compose one of your own.

Sky Trail

To think of a hiking trail as a friend and guru can seem odd, but for 20 years, one such place in the wilderness has been that for me. For six of those years I trekked Sky Trail four or five times a week, all year long, in rain, fog, sun, wind, under moon and in total darkness. I came to it depressed, angry, sad, buoyant, down with cold, wounded in knee, sore in back, sick with anxiety, juiced with excitement, and joyous. Human friends, preoccupied with their own lives, sometimes shunned me during the harder of these times. My angst stirred them too much, I guess, so they were no more available to me than the distant Farallon Islands, visible out in the Pacific on clear days from Inverness Ridge. The trail, though, was always there, whatever the trouble, whatever the time, steady as stone, alive to the beat and swing of my body, receiving my monologues, offering refuge from a busy, noisy world.

Like Zen masters I'd practiced with, this trail did not absorb my sufferings but rather showed by example the possibilities inherent in being total. It showed how to lead with heart and

9

see soul in every moment, in every activity, in every perception. The Zen master could do this because he truly knew himself, and, knowing himself, decided to take the Bodhisattva fork in the road—choosing not to use this knowing just for his own salvation but also to help others. Entering his chambers was like being in a room with mirrors on opposite walls, like being in my parents' bedroom when I was young and, looking into one mirror, seeing image after image of myself receding into infinity. Looking into the Zen master's eyes, I could not escape myself. This is true of the trail as well.

Sky Trail. A name that I'm sure someone thought reflected its altitude, with panoramic views of the bay, estuaries, and Pacific Ocean from the highest points. But to me the name Sky Trail is more about boundaries and limits, and specifically the lack of these. In human terms and conventions, Sky Trail has a beginning and an end—but it truly has no limits. Trail signs measure its distances from point to point, and lines on maps delineate its topography and boundaries, but the true nature of this trail is connoted by its name.

How can a human being come to rely on and trust such a trail for comfort, sustenance, even advice? If John Gray's cosmology is correct and men are from Mars and women Venus, what planet would a trail be from? Perhaps Earth. Yes, the trail is Earth itself, and it has a language all its own—a language ripened after millions of years. But it has more than a language, more than something that changes and evolves. It has a core, an essence that does not and never will waver. That marrow draws me to this trail and gives me hope that my own essence, sequestered somewhere inside me, may someday blossom in full light.

On Sky Trail, I've seen glimpses of this core of me that connects me so completely to all of life. There, the thinking mind often quiets enough that I begin to notice my feet walking and supporting my upright body (a great blessing to be aware of such an ancient and decidedly human activity!). I notice my breathing on the uphill sections. The weight of my body is less burdensome on my forward momentum as my arms swing like pistons powering me upward. As I sustain the connection with the trail, time stops. Real walking begins.

Stopping time. It has happened a few times, especially during most of four years at the end of the 1970s when I lived alone in my remote cabin in the New Hampshire woods, when the pace of life slowed as if each day was like writing a letter to a friend with pen and elegant paper, when no television measured my moments in 30- or 60-minute intervals. It's happened with lovemaking, too, when sex and love were indistinguishable—just the loving, and with love, no intrusion of time.

~

How has this relationship with a trail happened? After all, I do hike other trails and am at times equally intimate with them. Why do I think of Sky before all others? Others are more beautiful, easier to walk, more open to the sun and wind, closer to the ocean, have rushing water, are more famous, guarantee wildlife viewing, and have fewer flies, bats, and crows—but when I walk the Sky, I am more available to myself. My feelings are more on the surface, ready to be felt and understood. My body is challenged, but not so much that I become preoccupied with its protestations. Most importantly, there is something about this particular trail that cares for my soul. It is not that I go there to get something for my soul, but rather to be immersed in the calmness I feel just from being there. In a way, the trail is a caretaker for my soul, akin to Thomas Moore's description from *Care of the Soul* about the medieval practice of going to a garden when in a saturnine mood. One didn't retreat there to get something—to get rid of depression or melancholy—but to honor the feeling.

Not all places, wild or cultivated, allow this. But when you find a spot where time seems suspended, you may have arrived. God resides there. Not the God of our ancestors, with his flowing beard and robe, but the God of our own soul, the God who lives within and is always looking for an opportunity to reunite us with our soul home and spark our connection to life. For me, Sky Trail is a soul home where God and I can talk without distractions. The only obstacles to overcome are those within my mind—those clenched, white-knuckled corners where nothing lives, where feelings lie dormant, unacknowledged, festering, decaying, dead in the dark. Yet not far from those dark corners is a place where everything lives, has always lived, and will always live. How can this be?

Walking Sky Trail over these past years, I found answers and resurrected those dead emotions. Some of those answers came not in the form of words but simply from the cadence of my steps. Others came from the trail and demonstrated that death and life are intertwined, laced together like a doily and just as delicate. The Bishop pine near the trailhead, once so handsome against the dusk sky, so vibrant with jays, quail, finches, an owl from time to time, now dead, blackened, prostrate, uprooted, the victim of a 1995 firestorm so intense that it created its own wind, which fanned its own fire. Bishop pines need fire to maintain continual growth, otherwise they die out. The pine's cones, seared and rendered by the heat, exploded seeds like benign shrapnel to keep the species growing and healthy. Now, life sprouts around this dead tree like children encircling and honoring their grandfather. The small stands here are the last such wild Bishop pines left on the West Coast.

If I were walking Sky Trail for the first time today, I would not know this tree's story. I would see it only as it is now and would pass by, unaffected. Just another downed and dead tree in the forest. But the pine is an old friend, now gone, and I grieved its death after a long time knowing and appreciating and honoring.

There is so much to learn from Teacher Trail. Death grows the forest. Without it, all life would eventually suffocate and starve, or grow stunted. Over the years, our relationship has deepened. Its landscape affects me, stirs feelings, thoughts, actions, and my inner landscape—the amalgam of perception and personality shaped by my history and experience— affects it and all the forest around it. I go there consciously and care for its appearance as I do my own. I help keep it clean and orderly, picking up litter, removing a fallen branch, observing the rules of its road. From time to time I've acted as game warden, ranger, guide, chronicler, and forager. I've rescued birds; photographed bobcats, deer, jackrabbits, mushrooms, and skunks; admonished out-of-bounds bicyclists and dog walkers; guided other hikers; and picked huckleberries. I've picnicked there scores of times, danced the ancient Tai Chi on its mountaintops, stalked its deer with camera and binoculars, and snoozed away more than a few afternoons on its sunny meadows. I've hiked there in the early morning before dawn, in the noonday sun, at night under a moon so bright I could see my shadow, and on new-moon nights so dark I couldn't see my feet.

Yet I've done all these on other trails at other times. What makes this trail so sacred to me? It's that when I begin the trail a certain ease embraces me. A certain ease. How to define this? Regardless of how I may have disturbed an otherwise tranquil mind that day, the mere anticipation of going to the trail evens me out the way noodling with my guitar, or taking a nap on a lazy Sunday afternoon, or sipping a cold beer on a hot summer day might. But Sky Trail is much better than those, and its salvation far, far deeper.

Sky Trail is a place where I trust myself. I don't have to check on myself there and ask myself if I'm being myself. I just am who I am—a walker who at that moment in time is a part of the trail. I can never be as much a part of the trail as the lupine, or iris, or coyote bush, or fence lizard, or lumbering stink beetle, but I can live without being a burden to myself, without all the time wondering how I'm doing. Few places allow me to be as much myself as here. Perhaps one or two people in my 50-plus years fit that unique bill, offering safety, trust, comfortableness, acceptance. And as with those people, I return often to Sky Trail.

At times, I walk the trail slowly, like Thoreau's "...Sainte-Terrer, a Saunterer, a Holy-Lander." In "Walking," from his *Natural History Essays,* he goes on to say, "They who never go to the Holy Land in their walks, as they pretend, are indeed mere idlers and vagabonds: but they who do go there are saunterers in the good sense, such as I mean." At these times, I am unafraid, regardless of storm or wind or torrent or darkness. Without fear, I am hopeful, peaceful, loving, and full of interest and passion. I am not consumed with myself—my worries, my shortcomings, my successes, my failures. I am aware of not feeling as burdened, of not creating suffering for myself in that moment, of being present, without even defining it as "being in the now" or, indeed, "being present."

Without "my story" to preoccupy me, I can see the trail more completely. A monarch butterfly sips nectar on a thistle flower on a midsummer's day. A family of quail crosses the trail like harried commuters in Grand Central Station. The palette of rich greens and browns and blues gathers after a winter storm. The tiny tick on my leg, planning a juicy meal but not yet embedded and engorged (yes, seeing can save one from suffering at times).

That deep embrace of selfless seeing touches all life in the universe. Buddha experienced it sitting under a fig tree in India. He embraced all life, and we are still feeling the repercussions. Moses demonstrated boundless faith and courage in leading his people to a more hopeful life. Jesus taught through parables and personal example and we still feel the heat of his love. On the night before Martin Luther King Jr. was shot in Memphis, he told us that he had gone to the mountaintop for the sake of freedom—not for his sake, but ours—and we still feel his strong faith and selfless sacrifice.

With that embrace of selfless seeing, death is obliterated and life reaffirmed. Quietly, like the final stitch in an elegant embroidery, life is affirmed. The trail appears the same, as does the sky, the distant ocean, the forest, the flowers and mushrooms, yet the view is a wider and deeper one. Everything has changed.

~

You needn't come to Sky Trail to experience this. The trail I describe is not an obvious spiritual landmark like Mecca or Lourdes or the Wailing Wall or the Potala Palace. On this trail is where I find grace, but it may not be that place for you. With some careful searching, you can discover your own place, for what determines its sacredness is your relationship to it. As with the search for a soul mate, you have to circulate, to get out and explore. Hike around. See what feels special. Look to your heart for guidance and direction, and transplant your mind into your feet. Your own soul trail may not be deep in the wilderness. It may not be quiet or forested or even all that beautiful. It may be nearby.

Wherever that place, the benefits of visiting it are vast. So few places or people offer us the royal reception of receiving us no matter how foul our frame of mind. Sky Trail has never turned me away, has never refused to hear me out, has never said, "No, not today." A friend of mine who is going through a nasty divorce told me recently that her teenage daughter refused to return to a therapist because she was too vulnerable to reject the advice he was giving her. That young woman was wise indeed. Sky Trail honors my vulnerability and lets me find the courage to face my own feelings.

It listens as I walk—listens not as human beings listen, but to the beat of my feet. The late theologian and Zen popularizer Alan Watts said that the universe swings in rhythm like the beat of the human heart, and the trail listens for the music within me through the cadence of my step. I've met only one human being who could listen like that: the Zen master Sasaki Roshi, who knew exactly the nature of my mind and heart the moment I entered the Mount Baldy Zen Center *sanzen* (interview) room, where he sat like a living mountain waiting to test how open my heart and how empty my mind had become.

As in *sanzen*, so too on the trail. I can't escape from myself. Its distractions are not intoxicating enough to pull me away from my ungovernable feelings. The irony is that, in facing myself fully, I can let go of my self-consciousness and open to a larger Self, a Self that is permanent and eternal, a Self that is common to all living things, a Self that when touched brings me into communion with all life.

To guide me to that point—and that is the Zen master's ultimate goal—Sasaki Roshi employed only one prop in the *sanzen* interview room: a single flower in an unassuming vase. I do not remember what kind of flower it was, only that he asked me time and again, "How can you realize the flower?" This was my koan, the puzzle I had to answer not with my mind but with my heart and soul. I looked at the flower, then back at Roshi. It was not a situation where I could get back to him later with an answer. Nor could I launch into an intellectual explanation of my relationship with flowers in general. No, if I hesitated, Roshi would ring the little bell he kept at his side and dismiss me on the spot. My answer had to be as genuine as he was with me.

How can I realize the flower? How can I live this life with complete faith? How can I not only walk on the trail, but also embrace it so deeply that the line of separation between the earth and my boots becomes a blur, leaving nothing between us but love itself?

EXPLORING YOUR PATH

> Is there a place in nature that you are drawn to? A place that comes to mind if you try to imagine a place where you would feel relaxed? A place where you would choose to be if you had only a short time to live? Sit in a comfortable chair, close your eyes, and go to that place in your mind's eye. Imagine its smells, the way it looks in different light at different times of the year, the sounds, the textures of the flora, the lay of the land, its waters, rocks, trees, and every view it may have of the surrounding landscape.

> Spend a few minutes imagining all the facets of this special place. How do you feel after imagining this place? What comes to mind? Is your mind calmer? Do you yearn to go there? What do you do when you are there?

> In a journal, record your thoughts, feelings, and memories of this favorite place.

> Don't have a favorite place yet? Make one up, and imagine what it would look like, where it would be, and what you would be doing there.

The Living Trail

Sky Trail has hosted many who have come with questions, problems, blessings, desires, and dreams. Ten thousand years ago, the Miwok people who migrated across the Aleutian land bridge looking for a better life occupied this land and held it sacred. In 1579, when Sir Francis Drake, the first European to explore the area, sailed into nearby Drake's Bay, one of his men called this land "a goodly country, and fruitfull soyle, stored with many blessing fit for the use of man." Later, Spanish settlers and missionaries, taking advantage of the good climate and rolling hills, introduced agriculture and cattle ranching, which was continued by the Mexicans who followed. And in the mid-nineteenth century, after the United States acquired the territory, horse-drawn wagons followed the trail's rutted surface to bring milk and butter from dairy ranches to feed the growing population of Yerba Buena, that "good herb" of a town that was later rechristened San Francisco.

Was I too attracted to this area for its peace and abundance? It seemed a fertile ground where I could perhaps find roots and purpose. The trail and the forest had seen so many migrations but had turned no one away.

A trail as support? Why not? Perhaps I could develop my own creation myth around it—a Western version of Coyote and Hummingbird and Eagle that would involve the Snake of Divorce, the Owl of Anxiety, the Vulture of Depression, the Skunk of Isolation, and the Old Pine Tree of Death and Resurrection—and create a context for how I had come to this trail out of my own history and the civilization of the late twentieth century. My walking would then have purpose and would anchor me through times of dizzying change and uncertainty.

At 50, I became aware of a lack of roots, of connection, of an emptiness that was growing wider and deeper. How had I arrived at my present station? How had I lost my way? The trail was a messenger, a map that would lead me to internal places of mystery and discovery, places of origin I had lost touch with in the workaday world of achievement, ambition, and routine. Meeting a trail that seemed to offer such treasures and allowed me a loving, nonjudgmental setting for self-exploration led me to spend a lot of time with it.

Of course, humans are an integral part of the trail because we create trails and roads for commerce, expediency, or recreation. And because we are responsible for what we start, we are also responsible, not for the control of nature, but for its care, especially where our trails have changed the ecosystem. We often intervene in nature to expedite or profit our lives but don't realize the short and long-term effects. But trails require intelligence, attention, and concern. They demand that we work much more in partnership, rather than in the misconstrued stewardship of the Bible.

Western peoples, essentially removed from nature, are grop-
ing for roots. As a counselor and social worker, I've seen the
effects of the extremes of this rootlessness. For example, I
worked extensively with one man who was schizophrenic and
addicted to street drugs and alcohol but who nonetheless possessed a kind and sensitive heart. He never knew his biological
parents—the epitome of human rootlessness. He had been
abandoned at birth and at almost 50 was deeply psychotic and
at tremendous risk. His obsession and obvious suffering over his
abandonment contributed to a continual mental disorientation
that resulted in homelessness, flirtations with physical and mental collapse, and death, either from suicide or from drug and
alcohol abuse.

Like the human heart, a trail, too, if abandoned and
unmaintained, will succumb to bush and bramble, vine and thistle, weather and erosion, and will lose its identity and distinc-
tiveness. This is not a problem for the essence of the forest,
which knows no limits called "trails" or "roads" and will grow
in any neglected place, including freeways, parking lots, old
roads, railroad beds, and barren Hollywood sets. A trail in good
repair after a hundred years has obviously been greatly valued by
humans as a much needed route for trade, transportation, recreation, or pilgrimage.

~

Documentation of the Point Reyes peninsula didn't start until
the English and Spanish came, but we know from their writings
that the Miwok people used the ridge traversed by Sky Trail to
hunt game, particularly elk, and so followed the lines of the

topography to make their travel easier. They lived in a settlement below in a lush creek-fed valley now called Olema, a Miwok word for coyote, a milder, less windy place than the ridge and coastal dunes to the west.

A more definitive history of the entire peninsula began in the 1850s with the discovery of gold in the Sierra foothills. Miners with windfalls on their minds poured into California. The whole country was flexing its Lewis and Clark muscles, building railroads, encouraging westward expansion—and also forgetting Thomas Jefferson's words "that all men are created equal"—stripping Native Americans of their legal rights, denying them their ancestral lands, and rejecting that they were "endowed by their Creator with certain unalienable rights, that among these are life, liberty and the pursuit of happiness." In what Bay Area historian Malcolm Margolin, in *The Ohlone Way*, called "one of the ugliest episodes in American history," miners showed "...nothing but contempt and disgust, and the outright murder of thousands of California Indians in the middle of the nineteenth century." San Francisco became a bustling city that was both a stepping-off point for the hopeful and a refuge for the down-and-out.

Statehood soon followed, and Americans snatched back Mexican land grants that had been held since the 1820s, when Mexico won the territory from Spain. Land developers carved up the parcels and sold them to the highest bidders. The climate of the Point Reyes peninsula—dense summer fog and average temperatures in the low 50s throughout all four seasons—made the land more suitable to ranching than to farming. A San Francisco law firm headed by the Shafter family bought most of the land on the odd, forested peninsula that, separated from the mainland by pristine Tomales Bay and the San Andreas Fault, is actually on a different continent geologically. The firm leased a number of dairy ranches and unceremoniously named each one with a letter of the alphabet from A through Z to facilitate accounting procedures. Pioneer ranchers developed wagon trails to connect first with neighbors and then with more traveled roads to get their goods, particularly their much-prized and nationally distributed butter, to market in San Francisco. Sky Trail, one of those ranch roads, grew wider as frequent wagon traffic trampled down vegetation.

As for the trail's name, we know that the Miwoks didn't name it, nor did the Park Service. We do know that the Z Ranch, which was on the Sky Trail at Sky Camp, was once known as Sky Ranch, but we don't know who gave it that name, or exactly when. When I say "we," I mean myself and the people I asked—a knowledgeable park historian who also knew that a section of the trail from the trailhead to the ranch used to be known as the Fox Trail for Ann Fox, a popular local outdoorswoman; the wife of a former ranch employee who worked there from 1949 to 1962 and who remembered that the trail was called Sky before the park was created in 1962; the daughter of the ranch's foreman; an environmental activist who helped save the Point Reyes peninsula from development; an administrator in the Point Reyes National Seashore Association; the head of trail maintenance; and a trails keeper who had been around since the creation of the park. Nobody had any definitive answers, but, because I appreciate the mysteries and vagaries of natural things, I find the fact that no one knows who named the Sky entirely appropriate and satisfying.

In earlier days of the Spanish and Mexican rancheros, the hills around Sky Trail were mostly bare knolls, the result of cattle chewing and trampling anything tasty and green. The Z Ranch included the slopes just below Inverness Ridge and Mount Wittenberg. Wittenberg, the highest point on the peninsula, was named after the family that eventually bought the property from the Shafter law firm. Wind and weather kept growth in check as well, but it was mainly the grazing that shaved the vegetation to a buzz cut. Point Reyes historian Dewey Livingston points out the area was never logged and surmises that the Douglas fir forest that now graces the ridge took root after 1962, when Congress authorized the park and grazing ended.

The creation of the park also provided protections that began to restore some of its original wild diversity and abundance. Starting in the nineteenth century, opportunists had nearly full societal sanction to exploit and kill at will, and to push to extinction whatever flora or fauna they could profit from or that threatened their commercial interests. So big game (is hunting just a big game?) like elk and bear soon disappeared. The wildcats, cougars, and coyotes that threatened livestock also had to go. Waterbirds such as egrets were slaughtered en masse by greedy hunters to supply feathers for fashionable ladies' hats. And cormorants and other seabirds were decimated by poachers who sailed the 20 miles to the Farallon Islands to steal millions of eggs from the birds' nesting and breeding grounds. After all, hungry San Franciscans had to have their morning eggs.

~

Today, with federal and state protections in place, deer, coyotes, elk, badgers, bobcats, foxes, and even cougars have repopulated the peninsula. Songbirds, seabirds—including the once near-extinct cormorants and egrets—abound, along with great horned and spotted owls, hawks, ospreys, vultures, golden eagles, kites, brown and white pelicans, and some of the largest numbers and species of waterfowl on the Pacific Flyway migration path. Even a member of the black bear family that used to keep the Miwoks on their toes has been spotted. Off Sky Trail, coyote bush and purple and white lupine dominate the chaparral, while among the principal trees are pine (including the rare Bishop, a hardy maritime-loving species), bay laurel, madrone, and Douglas fir. During my Sky Trail hikes, I've seen most of this wildlife, and even Tule elk, which the Park Service introduced into the area between the ridge and the ocean in an effort to expand the existing herd on Tomales Point to the north.

Sky Trail roughly bisects the spine of Inverness Ridge, the range of coastal hills that rises like a humpback whale at Mount Wittenberg. The area I usually hike, which varies from three to 15 feet in width, passes through Sky Camp and loops around to the open meadows at the base of Wittenberg. Sky Camp is one of the park's four backcountry campsites. It is the site of the old Z Ranch, as evidenced by several huge antebellum cedar trees that were originally planted as wind breaks. Near Sky Camp is a spring and a creek that once serviced the old ranch. For years I stopped there to fill my water bottle—until a couple of years ago when the Park Service posted it unfit for drinking (joining an increasing number of contaminated springs in the West).

This entire "island in time," as nature writer Harold Gilliam called the Point Reyes peninsula in his book of that title, occasionally lurches northwestward with a major earthquake every

100 years or so. The most recent, the estimated 8.0 quake that devastated San Francisco in 1906, shook Point Reyes loose. A number of buildings and a train toppled over in the nearby town of Point Reyes Station, but a cow that fell into a chasm created by the quake was the only local fatality. Geologists soon discovered that the peninsula lurched 17 feet towards Seattle, something of a world record in the tectonic-plate Olympics.

In September 1962, President John F. Kennedy cited "the importance of saving and protecting a portion of the diminishing undeveloped coastline of the United States" when he signed legislation to authorize the establishment of Point Reyes National Seashore. The legislation followed a bitter battle to rescue the area from land developers who had already built houses on a gorgeous stretch of dunes called Limantour Spit, about five miles west of Sky Trail. Thanks to the efforts of a coalition of environmentalists, politicians, and ranchers, the federal government acquired that land, compensated the owners, and tore down the houses. In doing do, they helped preserve a national treasure. A number of the old dairy ranches, mostly in the northern end of the peninsula and separated from the wilderness areas of the park, are intact and still produce and sell quality dairy products through a local cooperative. Their owners profited greatly when the government paid them to agree to not sell their land to developers.

Because of all this cooperation and creative ecopolitics, we can now hike Sky Trail in perpetuity, instead of strolling or driving along some developer-dubbed "Sky Avenue" surrounded by houses and a golf course.

EXPLORING YOUR PATH

> Spend a few minutes thinking about a difficult life transition you have experienced. In your journal, describe what happened, then focus on where you found solace and support. Did you go to a particular place? Turn to particular people?

> Do you seek nature—the wild, your garden, a natural recreational area a town park—for emotional support? If you do, describe this place and how it helps you. If not, spend a few minutes envisioning such a place and write about how you could benefit from it.

> Do you know about any wild places in your state that need protection and preservation? Could you contribute to saving it? How might you do that? List such places and how you might help them.

Quietening

The seasonal changes on Sky Trail were softer and more subtle than in my New Hampshire home. Fall was no riot of color. Few deciduous leaves crackled underfoot. The night air was scarcely cooler than the day's, and because the fog tended to dissipate in the fall, that season was often the hottest of the year. The first rain of late autumn often fell like feathers, just slightly more than a spray providing relief from six months of the dry season, as Californians call it. This rainless time of year is unsettling for a Northeasterner used to distinctly defined seasons and the possibility of precipitation at any time of year. The first rain heralded the harder rains to come quietly, more like a clarinet than a trumpet. You could almost hear the parched brown hills of summer on the North American side of the fault sponge up the moisture. And on this Pacific "continent," greens deepened and mushrooms stirred beneath the pine and fir duff. First rain was soft and open like a kitten's belly, cool and moist, as light as duck down. And it usually lasted long enough to wet my cap and shrink it some—I've lost more caps to first California fall rains that have sneaked up on me like playful children.

First rains softened the edges of my emotions, and in 1988, my emotions were about as raw as an open blister. After five years of marriage, my relationship with Anita was on the verge of collapse.

~

Any serious relationship, but particularly a marriage, is a spiritual path, or at least can be. All the elements are there: attraction, inspiration, interest, discipline, effort, determination, concentration, communication, silence, time together, time alone, pain, pleasure, desire, joy, frustration, faith, and a willingness to surrender something of oneself to a higher calling—the calling of love. Tough times can either help it go deeper, or break it up. Sometimes, during the span of one day, you're riding the wind in a glider or drifting on rough seas without a rudder or flying into the eye of a storm.

At first, things had gone well. Harmony and peace prevailed. However, as the Buddha said in one of his first discourses after his Great Enlightenment (though I'm sure that thousands of Jewish grandmothers had said it before him), "Things change." Little things. Annoying things. Grating things. Things that didn't even seem like things but became things as our relationship went downhill. In *Soul Mates*, Thomas Moore, wrote about "…the tendency of people in a relationship to assume that psychological life is simple….In a soulful relationship, in contrast, the partners know that we are all individuals, with our own kind of richness that may not be fully and plainly revealed in daily life, and that an intimate relationship demands a courageous and openhearted acknowledgment of differences."

Unfortunately, Anita and I had a vested interest in sameness, and any hint of difference was interpreted as a threat to our marriage's fragile emotional foundations.   For human beings, sameness is suffocating and may be a major cause of our high divorce rate and our difficulty in sustaining monogamous relationships. Some people choose affairs. I chose Sky Trail, where I saw that diversity and differences led to vibrant growth. My affair was with Sky Trail and its dazzling array of species, weather, terrain, color, smells, views, and surprise events like wildlife sightings and spring wildflowers that arrived late and stayed into summer. It nurtured me while the marriage, with its droning predictability, drained me.

Things change. Sometimes for the better, like cleaner air in Pittsburgh or less crime in New York City. Not so our marriage. Slowly, Anita and I began to go our separate ways even inside our own house. I slumped into a depression that painted everything trashcan-gray. I saw no way out, so I didn't try to initiate any constructive solutions. I did what I had done for years when overwhelmed by difficult feelings: I got very quiet. I got clinically quiet. I took every opportunity to be away from her and home, and I retreated whenever possible to my confessional trail—venting, talking out loud to anything alive, lamenting, crying, begging for answers, wishing it all otherwise.

It was late winter and iris buds were already swelling and waiting for the first stretch of dry, warm days to blossom. California was desiccated—sucked dry by seven years of drought. Reservoirs had begun to look like mud holes, but in 1988 the drought showed signs of easing. The rains had been more frequent and sustained, and the hills were green with clover, purple with lacy velvet grass, and filigreed with silver hairgrass and quaking and rattlesnake grass, their dangling panicles shaking in the wind like a rattler's tail. Even the sparse, drought-resistant, native perennial bunchgrasses that had been eaten and trampled by grazing cattle and choked off by the European annuals, were thriving with the added rain.

These grasses and flowers and clover fed my soul as I ambled along, sometimes on the trail, sometimes off, letting nature enter me than I entered it. There, I literally "took a breather" and discovered what that phrase meant. At home, despite my years of breath-awareness meditation practice, which was intended to lead to mindfulness, I would forget my breath and become lost in dark, self-absorbed moods. On the trail, as I saw the result of a forest breathing and sharing that same air with plants and wildlife, I would "realize the flower," as Sasaki Roshi had demanded of me, and settle into natural rhythms along with everything else that breathes.

~

On Sky Trail, I could see the enormous growth that occurred when no ego was present. No judgment, blame, or retribution happened there. When change did come, as the result of fire, storm, drought, wind, or erosion, nothing resisted the reality of that change. And predation and natural destruction were also part of the grand design of growth, fecundity, and decay.

I went to Sky Trail often, for the deep healing the trail offered me, after our marriage ended that July. Anita and I began a struggle over possession of our house, and I withdrew even more, looking for respite from these difficult battles. For much of that summer, I walked in fog, that "grand and far-reaching affair," as John Muir described it. The fog fostered my inward mood. The cold and damp weren't my preference, but on Sky Trail in summer you take what's there or go inland for sun. On rare days, Sky Trail lay above the gray fog that pooled between the ridge and the ocean, and the sun would blaze, though its heat was cooled by the fog-created wind. That summer, sunshine on the coast was a benediction, a gift that lifted my spirit in that time of pain, recovery, and renewal.

Sky Trail softened the emotional rawness that lingered after our marriage ended. Its huckleberries, lupine, deer, pine, fir, ospreys, oak, quail, jackrabbits, hawks, bobcats all lived together in a tapestry of relationships, authentic, nonjudgmental, being themselves in as total a way as possible. In that environment, I could begin to heal, not through self-analysis but by seeing my True Self—that fully alive part of me that connected me to every other living thing, that part of me that was there before my birth and will be there after my death—reflected in a forest that expressed with no wasted effort, no lamentations, no remorse, no retribution, no tears, no tangles.

I saw why Native Americans held all of nature sacred, for the sacred bypasses the discriminating, categorizing, labeling brain and enters the soul directly through the senses. The plants and animals of the trail offered me refuge, a literal "fleeing back" to the natural, the spiritual, the sensuous, the real. They offered common ground where I could plant my feet and know (an earthquake notwithstanding) that it would not crumble, as had the emotional ground of our marriage.

~

Walking Sky Trail represented my own life journey. With its trailhead, forks and spurs, hills and vales, rises and dips, its summit, I could see similarities and landmarks related to my life. It offered a base that sustained me as other human bases collapsed, and I could retreat there to remind myself of a part of life that is forever constant and calm and alive, even amid change and uncertainty.

During my time in my New Hampshire cabin, the pace of life had slowed to synchronize with the pace of nature. I chopped wood and carried water and watched the day turn to night, and thought little about where my life was going because it was already there. The present moment was so fulfilling that I needed neither external stimuli nor internal planning to make life worth living. Life by itself was worth living, because nothing needed to be added. Living there in communion with the land, I learned to see. I learned to love walking and the taking-in of all around me that no other mode of transportation afforded. From nature, I learned about lightening my emotional load, about letting go of dense, burdensome thoughts, and of appreciating each day as a precious gemstone.

After discovering Sky Trail, I usually hiked it alone, either on short, five-mile aerobic jaunts, or, when time allowed, on long, strenuous day trips of 10- or 12-mile loops that covered the Coast Trail as well.

My inner landscape, my way of sensing and experiencing the world, needed silent time to discover what was there. "The most important language to learn to read is the language of the heart," wrote Algonquin descendant Evan T. Pritchard in *No Word for Time*. "You have to find your own answers, perhaps by slowing down and letting spirit catch up to you." Most of our vocations, recreation, and education involve so much activity and talk that when they stop, we are lost and fear overtakes us.

It isn't the fear of bobcats and cougars and bears and stormy weather that keeps most of us from spending time in nature. Rather, it's the fear of silence that stalks us like a dark, moving shadow in the moonlight. Most of us avoid that silence and wrap ourselves in "surround sound" even though we're somehow attracted, on deeper, unconscious levels, to Gregorian and Tibetan chanting and the practices of meditation, prayer, and contemplation. In silence, we have a greater chance of catching a glimpse of our True Self, but this can be a scary thought for minds consumed with daily practicalities and logistics that have nothing to do with who we truly are.

On the trail, as I walked alone in the cool of late fall, fog and drizzle muffled any forest noise and I heard only the grunts and shuffles my body made chugging up hills. In the silence, I saw for the first time the bright-red stems and twigs of the huckleberry plant and how it provided a stout infrastructure for its holly-green leaves. Once the berries were gone, I had overlooked the rest of the plant and its beauty against the roiling slate-gray fog. Beauty overlooked is life overlooked, and life wants only recognition—not just of the obvious, but also of the tiniest, the rancid, the pretty, the putrid.

As I admired the whole huckleberry plant, my mind began to settle. Such details are nature's devices for bringing us closer to the harmony of the forest. Talking, though perfectly natural to human beings, is not an inherent part of that harmony. To stop talking for a time, we must first consciously intend to be quiet, for talking can begin and continue habitually. To break the habit, at least for these moments on the trail, we must first become aware that we are talking or intend to talk. Otherwise, too often, talking never stops at all. It becomes an endless loop from the road to the trail to the summit back down the trail to the car to the road.

Although it meant sacrificing the silence, I did enjoy social times on the trail, especially with friends like Bob who were attuned to the spiritual value of being in nature. At some point in our conversations, one of us would frequently suggest that we spend some time in silence. This was not the imposed or contrived silence of a meditation retreat, but rather an acknowledgment of the kinship between us that needed no words to define or explain it. To be together and yet absorbed in our own being was to say, "I'm comfortable enough with you and trust you enough that I don't have to constantly be camouflaging myself with words, ideas, and responses. I can reveal who I am to you in silence, as the pine reveals itself to its neighbor fir over the years of silent growth." We would come out of our silence as naturally as we had entered it, feeling enlivened, continuing our laughing, advising, conjecturing, wisdom-ing, and clowning.

Walking quietly, I am sensitive to sounds "that thicken the sensory stew of our lives," as Diane Ackerman wrote in *A Natural History of the Senses*. The sounds of nature are consonant with the sounds of my body: the thump of my feet, the rustling of nylon against nylon or cotton, the gentle pounding of my heart up hills, the huff of air wheezing in and out like the "little engine that could" as it chugged up a steep grade. These are relatively unobtrusive sounds that blend with sparrow-song, crow-caw, wind-rush, tree-creak, and rain-patter, and the extraordinary song of the winter wren, a tiny bird that lives hidden in the Douglas fir understory and, in one 10-second breath, sings an aria that would put the best human lieder singers to shame. But when people pass by talking loudly, it's as jarring as hearing someone in the audience have a coughing spell during a performance of Ferde Grofe's *Grand Canyon Suite*. The human voice can express the most exquisite beauty at times—the Swingle Singers, the soft moans and endearments of lovers, the gentle words we offer when playing with our cat, the voice of a father expressing love to his child, Joan Baez, Aaron Neville, opera singer Ying Huang, the ballads of Nat King Cole—but when loud voices, as boisterous as Bourbon Street during Mardi Gras, suddenly pierce the silence on this pure path, the coarse noise, out of place, jars my ears. I am not advocating absolute silence on wilderness trails, for I know that humans are a talking lot, but if talkers were sensitive to others walking in what might be their own sacred trail, perhaps they would remember to lower their volume and modify their timbre. I may sound like a grumpy old man, but we have so few places left where quiet communion with nature is possible.

When all is quiet, I can hear what the noise obliterates, for, like a firestorm that whips up its own wind, the absence of noise can conjure up fear, which in turn conjures its own distinct sounds that torment and confuse, contract and tighten. For some people, like the schizophrenic and bipolar patients I've counseled, fear becomes a threatening inner voice that often shouts internal commands like a drill sergeant in the army. For me, too, fear has voices—though, thankfully, not psychotic ones. Descended as I am from a long line of warrior worriers, fear burns in my familial unconscious, and its theme of survival echoes through the centuries.

~

Perhaps that's why I'm drawn to this trail. It is more than a model of survival. As part of Gaia—environmental scientist James Lovelock's concept of a living and unified Earth—it has advanced to the level of support in that every event abets the commonwealth. A tree limb cracks in a storm. It falls, decays—and then supports future flora, feeds and houses insects, birds, reptiles, amphibians, and mammals, including humankind. A marsh hawk dives and digs its talons into a fat field mouse. That small murder helps to maintain the ideal balance of mouse to meadow to bobcat to jackrabbit to cougar to deer to grass to chaparral to fir to huckleberry to coyote. A fire, started by lightning, sears the understory. The devastation promotes new growth, which advances the health of the canopy and attracts songbirds, squirrels, owls, wood rats, caterpillars, and butterflies.

I once attempted to hike to the top of Half Dome in Yosemite from the valley floor in one day. This is a monstrous hike of about eight miles one way with an elevation gain of more than 4,000 feet. By the time I reached the base of the granite monolith where a Rube Goldberg-like collection of cables, poles, and wooden planks awaited my final ascent, I was exhausted. The grade equaled the steepest of San Francisco's streets, and I thought the climb impossible for me at that point. About halfway up, with my legs cramping and my energy almost spent, I was about to give up. But at that moment, a young girl who was descending came toward me. She was about 14 and truly an angel. She saw me struggling and called out to me, a complete stranger, "You can make it. Keep going. It's just a little farther," and I was inspired to continue and eventually realize the summit. I also discovered the community of that particular soul trail—on that day, human to human.

All aspects of nature, from a minuscule mushroom to mating elk, affect and influence everything else, including human beings. The Vietnamese Buddhist monk Thich Nhat Hanh calls this "Interbeing," which means simply that we are related to everything everywhere and at all times—that everything—every atom, molecule, neuron, cell, elephant, wildflower, soldier, cloud, affects every other thing, for better or for worse.

Interbeing means that we are responsible not only for ourselves but for every other thing in the universe. However overwhelming it may seem, our every act, no matter how base, noble, large or small we might think it is, affects everything around us. Each time I drive to Sky Trail, I no doubt kill many tiny beings. The turkey I ate last night (even if it was organically raised) once hunted and pecked around a barnyard. Just like any other warm-blooded being, it breathed, desired, ate, felt pain and pleasure. The hiking boots that carry me along the trail were made in a country that relies on child labor and denies basic liberties to its citizens.

~

I try to be aware of these consequences of actions, to minimize them, and to care for my planetary community. I try not to crush the large, black, wingless stink beetle that takes half a day to plod across what to it must be a vast tundra of a trail in search of food. In my New Hampshire cabin, I vowed to not kill anything for a year—not a fly, mosquito, mouse, or bug of any kind. This was not an easy vow to keep in a buzzing and biting New England spring and summer, but honoring life in that way was a powerful and sacred way to live. On Sky Trail, I extend the practice and vowed to never consciously step on or harm any other creature. Creatures in nature deserve to live as much as we humans do. Why would their lives be less valuable than ours? Certain species of ants can live up to 15 years—that's one single ant. Surely all living things deserve careful attention, protection, and consideration. I pick up a candy wrapper that someone has mindlessly discarded, and restore a bit of wildness. I remove a fallen branch, and clear the way for the next hiker. I bring an injured bird or lizard to a wildlife rescue center. These are not "random acts of kindness," as the bumper stickers say, but "small acts of awareness" and care that help to maintain the natural balance.

Because humans are the only species capable by themselves of upsetting that balance, an increase in consciousness among individuals, who often band together in conscious groups, can help to restore it. Witness the young environmental activist, Julia Butterfly Hill, who lived for almost two years at the top of an ancient 200-foot-tall redwood on a ridge in Northern California's coastal hills to protest plans for clear-cutting the remaining old-growth redwoods in the area. Witness Greenpeace dogging illegal whaling ships. Witness The Nature Conservancy buying and protecting chunks of wilderness near cities. Witness the creative plan to save the Amazon rain forest by developing a market for the exotic nuts that grow there. Witness a Sierra Club member joining a weekend crew to clean up a remote beach. Witness your neighbor, perhaps, recycling whatever possible and finding nontoxic alternatives to spreading poisons on lawns and gardens. The opportunities for enlightened action are vast, and each act is in the service of a cause much larger than the individual who carries it out.

The essence of Sky Trail, or any cathedral of nature, is found in the consciousness of every visitor. Each creates the trail anew with every fresh awareness, every sense that awakens, every step taken, every act of kindness and caring, every wild edible berry noticed, picked, and savored. *You Are the World*, Indian philosopher J. Krishnamurti titled one of his books, and each of us creates it moment by moment with our every word, thought, and action.

~

"How can you realize the flower?" Sasaki Roshi asks me. The question stops thought. How do I answer? I have no words, and, in having no words, fear arises. Surrounding the fear is silence. Between the flower and me is silence. Silence floods the *sanzen* room. The flower, Roshi, the space in the room, the universe swamps me. For the moment, I am immersed in the silence.

EXPLORING YOUR PATH

> Give yourself a few moments to experience silence. Find a comfortable spot and still your body. Focus on your breathing. Don't try to breathe a certain way. Just observe the rise and fall of your abdomen and the sensation of air entering and leaving through your nostrils. Do this for 30 seconds, or 10 minutes, or 30 minutes, or for however long you can. Sitting and watching your breath is a way you can introduce yourself to a silent part of you. Buddhists call it the True Self, and Christian contemplatives call it the language of God. What is this experience like for you?

> Every deed or word is preceded by an intention, a thought that we may seldom be aware of. Make it a point each day to "catch" your intentions before you act. If you can begin to catch your intentions, you'll find that you become more skillful and sensitive in your everyday relationships. After you become familiar with catching your intentions, experiment with this: Before every action, monitor the intention behind it and consider how your intention might affect the quality of the action. Buddhists call this Right Action, one aspect of the Noble Eightfold Path to Enlightenment.

> Take some time to recall your last experience with weather, be it snow, rain, hail, tornado, or the first nice day of spring, and write about your memories and feelings in your journal.

Faith in a Huckleberry

Beneath tall Douglas firs, at the start of Sky Trail, huckleberries grow. They are California huckleberries, which are not really huckleberries but a species of blueberry. No one seems to know that, though, and they've been called huckleberries for too many years for people to acknowledge they are actually blueberries. Huckleberries contain small pits, but these purple jewels have nothing of the kind to obstruct their taste, their whole taste, and nothing but their taste as their flesh touches the flesh of my lips, tongue and mouth. However, so as not to antagonize Northern Californians, I'll continue to call them "huckleberries." (That name, by the way, is an American derivative of the "whortleberry," which is derived from an even older name, the "hurtleberry," which comes from the Saxon *heortberg* or the "hart's berry," which relates to an old English word, hurts, used in heraldry for certain round objects on coats of arms that resembled hurtleberries). In the absence of fossil records, we can assume that huckleberries were not around when the Pacific Ocean floor first collided with the North American continent several hundred million years ago and formed the Point Reyes land mass. In fact, according to some estimates, 30 million years ago the peninsula was located about 350 miles farther south, in the southern Sierra Nevada Tehachapi Range, and its geologic origins may go back 140 million years, when sand, clay, and lime washed down and filled some shallow lagoon on the Mexican coast. In true California fashion, this spit of seemingly stable land moves two inches northwest every year, the geological equivalent of a cheetah's speed. In another 30 million years or so, it appears, Point Reyes fisher folk will find themselves sipping lattes (a drink that is sure to survive the ages) just outside Seattle.

Huckleberries likely arrived in the region soon after bracken ferns, one of the oldest plants known (and still extant in these parts). Both help to hold soil from washing away in storm floods. Chances are it was migrating birds from the north that brought stowaway huckleberry seeds to this land in their feathers, their talons, and their dung.

My admittedly unscientific interest weaves my own experience of seeing, touching, and picking with experiential research that proves how wild sweetness and blue-smeared fingers can transform a melancholic mood into a deeper bliss than any ever attained from any guru or psychoactive substance. Huckleberries, which ripen in the early fall and cluster near the trailhead and higher on Inverness Ridge, help to shut off, if only for a moment, my eternal critical self-chatter. They show me where I stand in relation to wild things.

African-Americans celebrate Kwanzaa, a holiday based on African harvest festivals that means "first fruit of the harvest" in Swahili. It honors their ancient roots, their culture, their values, and their families. Any first fruiting is an exciting event. I anticipated the berrying all summer long, watching the progressive stages, trying to beat the birds to the first taste. I'd stop and study the plants almost daily, looking for the color changes that signaled ripeness.

First fruit is round and ripe and ready. Likewise, the first fruiting of the California huckleberry reawakens us to the value of noticing and honoring small things—those "matters of fact" that we often ignore because we're too busy to bother. As the Greek philosopher Pliny said, "Nature exceeds in the least things." Hikers, myself included, come to the trail laden with thoughts and worries seeking a dose of nature, relief from city congestion, a vista, a look at the forest, a breath of fresh air. We come for respite from the dis-eases of this "dusty world," as the Taoists referred to the sometimes bewildering "world of 10,000 things." But how many of us drop our gaze from the grand views and stop to smell the wild, resinous bark of a Douglas fir or palm a pinecone or eyeball a slug or savor some miner's lettuce?

~

One day, when I was hiking with my friend Gregg Levoy, the author of *Callings,* he suddenly stopped and went silent. His gaze was transfixed on a stout, bare, burnt-sienna branch of a Pacific madrone. It was as if he had glimpsed a lover from long ago and been mesmerized, perhaps even stunned, by her lithe beauty and grace. Our brain can, of course, process extraordinary volumes of information simultaneously, but even it pauses at pure, virgin beauty and suddenly blossoms into love. The moment passed and we continued walking and talking, but

Gregg told me that at that moment he had experienced what the Greeks called *eucharistia*, or gratitude.

In that moment, he had found relief from his busy world as his eyes, consciousness, and being came into full relationship with that branch in a communion of two so free of thought that perhaps the whole sentient world felt it on some level. In that moment of silent Epiphany, Gregg was in love with the universe. We often overlook huckleberries and madrone branches, though, for we see them only in passing, in a blur, as our next step carries us away too fast, too soon, to see the possibilities of communion with all things that grow.

To see huckleberries, to hear them as if each teardrop white flower had a tiny bell clapper for a stamen, to see beaded dew on their rich, green leaves, requires a stopping—and not just a physical stopping, but a focusing of full attention on the plant, as the finch and fox do. To truly see a huckleberry is to transcend living meanly, the term Thoreau used as the opposite of his ideal of living sincerely. To live "deep and suck out all the marrow of life" requires an attitude of receptivity to what is alive, around, and, ultimately, within. To live meanly is to live the way corporations conduct business: balancing the books, coming out ahead, meeting deadlines, paying bills, downsizing, getting things accomplished, improving bottom lines, generating profit-and-loss statements, and often ignoring environmental and social considerations. To live sincerely means finding value in the details, the background, and the tiny events that can take place on a square inch of soil. All it requires is a mind that values and honors slowing down and observing, even in the middle of a busy day. In the film *A Thin Red Line*, based on James Jones's novel, a young soldier, in the heat of a terrible battle, looks up, notices, and touches a delicate fern growing on the battlefield. In that moment, the war vanishes and he is a child again, playing in a meadow in full relationship with something—alive. However close death is, life is closer.

~

It is early fall, clear and warm, and all through the fog-bound summer I've been watching the Huckleberry Follies unfold. New sienna stems, sprouting from firm woody branches, supporting leathery, holly-like, bright-green leaves, hosting delicate white flowers that birthed the green, then blue, then deep-purple berries. By virtue of their small size, huckleberries require me to surrender to the moment. To see them fully, I must suspend getting somewhere; I must modify schedule, plan, goal for that moment. Sometimes I cannot let go. Too much to do, not enough time. Even on weekends, distractions, obligations, responsibilities dominate the days. I start my walk and my mind jumps into action with its decisions and judgments: no time to go a-berrying today, or I must get home before nightfall, or I've got no food in the house and must go shopping before the stores close, or I forgot to set the VCR and can't miss *60 Minutes*. In those misguided moments, I judge huckleberry picking as less important than something else I need to accomplish that day. What is more important, though, than a moment of peace, of beauty, of mental respite?

One of my fondest and most enduring memories is lazing about on a New Hampshire mountain picking and eating blueberries, and then dozing through a hot July afternoon. That was over 20 years ago, but the memory is as vibrant as today, and it comforts me still. In those days, blueberries were a priority (although the word "priority" seems out of place, more suited to a workplace) and summer days, like the days of California Native Americans before Europeans arrived, revolved and evolved around the ephemeral fruiting season. "Blueberry pickin'," I wrote in a song back then, "All I want to do is pick 'em and eat 'em my whole life through." Attending to berries in that way, to those tiny, wild, natural, free things, was a way of balancing the busyness of life.

Stopping, observing, picking, eating, can suspend our awareness of the passage of time, and when our mind is not trammeled by time, moments of bliss and even grace can come that will imprint themselves in our memory forever. I get frightened by the fast passage of time, which the pace of my activities only seems to accelerate.

Years ago I went to a Buddhist monastery in the Santa Cruz Mountains south of San Francisco for a solo retreat where I spent three days in a tent. I lived most of that time watching day turn to night and night to day. Aside from a brief lunch and a walk, that was all I did. Boring, you might think, but they were delicious days. Stripped of everyday distractions, I settled into each day—simple, elegant, adagio, pianissimo.

Nowhere to go, nothing to do, as the American-born Buddhist monk Ajahn Sumedho often says, and in those few days I discovered for the first time the essence of a day—the subtle changes in temperature from before dawn to sunrise, the first bird singing the first song, the breeze at mid-morning, the calm of midday punctuated by the tapping at the woodpecker's workshop, the cessation of wind at dusk, the refrains of crickets quieting as evening progressed, the haunting call of a great horned owl at midnight and the hopeful answer from its mate, the dead-still silence of 3 A.M. smashing the last vestiges of external stimuli that my mind could cling to in its desperate attempt to avoid looking at itself. The soft, ethereal light of dawn. I observed how a day "spends" itself and realized how often I lived days in opposition to their true rhythms, hues, tones, and textures.

The Information Age places little value on such learning. If you typed "living a day" in your search engine, it would probably come up empty. Yet those days molded me like hands molding clay on a potter's wheel. In facing each day squarely, I faced myself as never before. I came to a new relationship with time. Perhaps it was only an illusion of perception, but I began to feel that I could control the speed of time's passage by the quality of attention I gave to each aspect of the day. Background and foreground, self and world, blurred into one continuous present.

The speed of time and the awareness of approaching death can still rattle my nerves, but the experience of living a day with undivided attention has brought me ease. If I knew I was to die next week, I would be fearful but not regretful about what I hadn't yet done. After living those days in all their fullness, I felt less driven to do, to accomplish. Our culture may view this as passive, but it was not that. On the contrary, I became more interested, alive, and aware of the small events that sustained and nourished my spirit as food did my body. At his retreats, Ajahn Sumedho often begins each day by speaking to his students not of enlightenment or nirvana or samadhi or any of the possible fruits of meditation, but of the day, of this life, itself. "Not complicating it by trying to add to it…" he explained in *Seeing the Way*, "…we're just being aware of it as it is."

Too much doing, too much desire, too much thought, too much planning, too much worry, too fast a pace—all these hound the spirit and make it flee into dark corners where it cowers and tries to restore itself with periods of retreat, silence, and prayer. Without these necessary palliatives, we become prisoners of time, and every day feels like a noose that tightens with every passing minute. Huckleberries and the world of grand minutiae around us help to unknot the noose and offer us glimpses into a world beyond anticipatory anxiety, deadlines, and "gotta run." They are tiny portals that open onto a view of our alive and true nature...if only we choose to see it.

To my knowledge, no one has heralded the spiritual benefits of huckleberries before, so my suppositions (unlike the fruit itself) may be hard to swallow. The point of contemplation is not so much the berry itself but the berrying: the noticing, stopping, beholding, observing, and, if ripe, eating. If you bring awareness to those actions, then you elevate the event to consciousness (unlike most human endeavors, which in effect resemble sleep), and anything brought to consciousness is a step up the ladder of spiritual evolution. In the absence of awareness, the berry remains just another commodity to be consumed, and we remain what the government and media have labeled us: consumers.

The word "consumer" always makes me think of the Buddhist "hungry ghosts"—suffering beings with gaping mouths, long skinny necks, and huge bellies that can never be filled—so much like shoppers pillaging until time, other obligations, or the announcement that the store will close in five minutes ends the orgy of consumption. The ad boys and their corporate clients herd us into pens, feed us choices of their choosing, and make us believe the choice is ours and that if we don't have or want what the guy next door has, we're a little weird, or at least deprived. The forces that plot and accomplish this pin the rationale for all their products and services on consumers, who, the planners claim, have demanded them. The fact is, most of us don't want harmful or useless products, but the producers have created the illusion that we do. And the result—a glut of garbage that people actually buy—makes profits for the entrepreneurs and the ad boys and girls, but ultimately a bloody mess of the environment and sometimes our lives.

~

Huckleberrying, and the state of mind it requires, changes all of that. You pick or observe or pass by. You are free to choose, to roam and explore outside the usual specious reality being stage-managed by the usual corporate and advertising industry suspects.

Henry David Thoreau was the greatest American proponent of huckleberries (and his New England variety was a true huckleberry). "When I see, as now, in climbing one of our hills, huckleberry and blueberry bushes bent to the ground with fruit," he wrote in "Huckleberries" from his *Natural History Essays*. "I think of them as fruits fit to grow on the most Olympian or heaven-pointing hills." Thoreau loved wild berries, and loving one part of nature, even a tiny part, with all your being, is tantamount to loving all of nature, all of the plant and animal world, all of humanity, all of the cosmos. "We pluck and eat in remembrance of her (Nature)," he continued. "It is a sort of sacrament—a communion—the not-forbidden fruits, which no serpent tempts us to eat. Slight and innocent savors which relate us to Nature, make us her guests, and entitle us to her regard and protection."

Slowing down and seeing what is before us is a simple enough concept. But the pace of our life is so fast that we usually act with little consciousness of the thoughts and feelings that precede our actions. We are, at our soul's depth, sensitive as well as sentient, perceiving beings, but how many of us can reflect on one day, or even one hour of a day, and recall the perceptions and sensations that led to our subsequent actions? The extreme of this is the addict, who has lost the ability to discriminate among thought, desire, and satisfying an urge, no matter how destructive. But do we not all have some of the addict in us?

~

Sky Trail was, and remains, an antidote to such mindlessness. Picking California huckleberries, purple and succulent, in late summer on the ridge beneath a canopy of Douglas fir, pine, and madrone, was like sipping a sumptuous cup of tea in a garden so beautiful it could only be imagined. In *The Flavors of Home*, Bay Area wilderness chef and attorney Margit Roos-Collins calls such picking "pleasant tedium" and sums up the experience as time well spent. "Because picking the berries is an accomplishment, no matter how small," she wrote, "it frees me from the feeling that I need to make the time count by thinking about something important or making plans. When I pick huckleberries, I just exist, like a kid floating through summer vacation."

EXPLORING YOUR PATH

> When was the last time you went to pick wild berries or some other wild edible? Well, it's time. Unless you live in the far north and are three feet deep in snow, go out and find some fruit to pick, be it in the wild or even at a pick-your-own farm or orchard. Let yourself become intimate with the fruit you eat. Then take a few minutes to record your impressions and feelings in your journal.

> Tomorrow morning, get up before sunrise and go to some accessible spot in nature where you can simply observe the changing of night to day. Open all your senses and experience this daily miracle that we so seldom see.

> Today, when you're smack in the middle of errands, work, chores, phone calls, and meals, just stop. Look around you and notice something in nature—clouds, distant hills, a chirping bird, the sound of a creek, the smell of pine needles, the feel of the wind. Take a few minutes to record what you noticed.

Fire on the Ridge

In October 1995, a terrible wildfire burned one-sixth of Point Reyes National Seashore's hundred square miles, including 50 homes on Inverness Ridge near Mount Vision, toward the northern end of the park. The blaze started when a small group of teenaged boys made an illegal campfire near Mount Vision—not, apparently, out of mischief but just for fun. When they left, they covered the embers and thought they had put the fire out, but the winds, whipping hard as they will in the fall, exposed and ignited the embers into a small fire and then into an uncontrollable blaze that swept along the ridge. By the time firefighters arrived, the fast-moving flames were attacking inaccessible hills and dales and burning thick underbrush that hadn't seen fire in more than half a century.

The day the fire broke out, I was in Santa Cruz, about a hundred miles to the south, relaxing and picnicking on a warm beach with my girlfriend, Lorraine. It was a couple of weeks before my fiftieth birthday, and I spent much of that afternoon lying on the beach in a kind of dreamy oblivion contemplating my future. I was completely unaware of the drama unfolding to the north. I did notice a smoky haze and a surreal orange halo around the sun, but all seemed well and love was in the air for us that day.

At one point, Lorraine had to leave and take care of some business, but I stayed and spent some restless time reflecting on my approaching birthday. Fifty felt like a lofty wall that I had no choice but to climb before my journey could continue, but at that point the challenge seemed insurmountable. For the previous eight months, I'd been working on a book proposal that I had hoped would jumpstart my flagging writing career. My previous book, *Sacred Paths and Muddy Places*, a personal account of the years I had spent living alone in my New Hampshire cabin and my eventual move back to urban life, a cross-country move to Berkeley, California, had gotten a few good reviews in smallish periodicals but never took off.

Money was getting tighter, and I was contemplating, with some dread, turning again to my master's degree in counseling to bail myself out by returning to the social services field. Jobs were usually available for counselors willing to work with people suffering from chronic mental illness. The work was low-paying, exhausting, and rather thankless, but it nonetheless always offered an income as well as the rewards of helping others. The cost, though, was felt emotionally and physically. And for me, the prospect of this work was daunting because I was in my own recovery from a panic disorder, a trauma that first hit in my early twenties when I was working in a state prison. Over the next seven years, the anxiety generalized to agoraphobia, which literally means "fear of open spaces" but translated for me into fear of just about everything.

After suffering much damage—vocationally, socially, emotionally, spiritually, and financially—I regained some control, mostly through desensitization therapy that involved a deconditioning process, and particularly through Buddhist insight meditation, a technique that required long periods of sitting still, back straight and legs crossed, while watching my breath and noting not the content of my experiences but the very processes of thinking and feeling. My meditation practice eliminated my panic attacks, although anxiety continued to plague me for years, and still does, when stress mounts.

Anxiety had robbed me of many moments of peace and happiness, and I felt that day, as I neared 50, that the sand was running too quickly through the hourglass. Still, as I sat under the warm California sun, I was able to keep my darker thoughts at bay, at least for a while.

That evening, we headed home to Inverness Park, a small town on the east side of Inverness Ridge. Lorraine was living with me on a short-term basis but would soon leave for India to further her meditation studies with Tibetan Buddhist teachers. During the drive we listened intently to reports about the fire. But we were unprepared for the sight that greeted us when we drove over the hill that led into Point Reyes Station, the main town in the national park area. Across fingerling Tomales Bay, all of Inverness Ridge was ablaze. A few days before, I'd been blithely picking huckleberries on that same ridge.

"Oh, my God!" was all I could say. We were both in semi-shock. All life on and around the ridge tightened and braced.

~

Fire not only changes life, it is inseparable from life, as the sun attests. Aboriginal peoples knew this; they used fire to control their environment and included it in their ceremonies. The natural world, too, evolved with fire as a periodic check on plant life that would otherwise outgrow itself. For the Bishop pine, fire would insure the survival of the species, which was in danger of extinction in its limited West Coast range. For the native blacktail deer, though, the fire brought fear and panic. Dairy ranchers on the Point Reyes headlands, near Drake's Bay reported seeing scores of deer swimming—and deer are normally not known to swim—to the safety of the other side's pastures. As for huckleberries, the ones on the ridge closest to where the inferno started burned and died, only to be replaced before long by yellow and purple tree lupine.

And the people fled, too, not swimming but in cars. No one was hurt or killed, but 50 homes—sanctuaries of accumulated memories and treasured possessions—burned on that one Sunday afternoon. For a year or so before the blaze, I'd been following the construction of a cantilevered masterpiece whenever I hiked into the area above my home. The house, which had a huge deck that overlooked the east side of Inverness Ridge, was almost complete. A master stonemason had been putting the finishing touches on two magnificent fieldstone chimneys, picking and placing each stone with the passion and precision of a sculptor. In just minutes, though, the house turned to rubble. Only the unfinished chimneys remained standing, like nineteenth-century gravestones. Days later, I saw the owner standing in the rubble like a stunned yet defiant general on a charred battlefield. "I'll build it again," he told me, kicking at the ash. "I'll build it again."

Driving up to our house that evening, we saw that it had-not burned yet. But the fire was only a quarter-mile away and smoke was swirling above us. This was no longer something I could watch from afar or on TV. Fire creates an urgency that focuses the mind quickly on what is necessary and meaningful. We had only seconds to decide what to take from what had taken each of us years to amass. The fire marshal was allowing only one trip in and out. What could I do without? What matter mattered most? I hammered out my choice: my laptop computer, my old-friend Guild six-string guitar, some family mementos, particularly a Laughing Buddha figurine that had belonged to my grandmother, a few treasured books, some clothing for the indeterminate evacuation. Left behind to the possible holocaust were the TV, the VCR, the stereo, kitchenware, files stuffed with the ancient and obsolete, clothing I hadn't worn in years. Most of what was left was bric-a-brac, a word I now understand as representing the flotsam and jetsam of life—the "stuff" I not only didn't need for my emotional and spiritual sustenance but that slowed me down like a ball and chain. In those moments of panic, the fire revealed a cut-away view of what I truly valued: about half a carload of essentials, my girlfriend, and my own life. Lorraine took only what was essential for her trip to India.

I valued, too, the natural world, a vital part of which was burning above, and I felt compelled to stay and help save it rather than running. As I watched the flames devil-dance on the ridge, the Iron John within me wanted to paint my face and enter the burning forest purified of all that was not real or true in my life. I wanted to sear away the remaining fear that blocked my full entry into that silent place within, where God was always present and available. I wanted to start my life over, like a sapling sprouting from a stump.

~

Sifting through my stuff spotlighted what was wild in my own nature—that part of me that, like the raging firestorm, created my own inner winds and stoked my life moment after moment. The sight of the fire destroying my beloved forest sickened me, but the flames also illuminated a part of my spirit that had lain dormant for years. Our spirit needs fire of some sort—heat, passion—to keep it alive. It needs that spark, and the air, wind, and flame that keep it alive, so we can get up and walk despite the weight of time, obligation, and difficulty. My first wife, Donna, killed herself not long after we parted because, I think, she lost the flame and couldn't regain it. Without that spark and the breath that will blow it into flame, she fell victim to boredom, depression, and hopelessness. She tried to rekindle the flame with prescription painkillers, and in my work as a counselor, I've seen others turn to alcohol, cocaine, speed, pot, crank, and tranquilizers—but all to no avail.

Despite my own troubles with anxiety in my younger years, I was able to avoid turning to drugs, drink, or psychotropic medications because I knew that after the initial relief I'd probably get hooked. I did become "addicted" to carrying around a five-milligram Valium pill wrapped in a tissue for can't-take-it-anymore, on-the-brink-of-oblivion panic attacks. When on rare occasions I swallowed it, I felt so good, so mellow and blissed-out, that all I wanted was to kick back, chill out, and bask in the absence of anxiety. But the pill also dulled the edge of my creative urges, which in my mid-twenties included writing, making music, and photography. Anxiety is not always a foe. It is the result of a conflict between tremendous feelings from the heart that naturally want acknowledgment and expression, and the ego as it tries to keep these feelings repressed, unperceived, and unfelt. This battle results in tension and stress that express themselves in the body as a racing heart, lightheadedness, cold hands, sweaty palms, a feeling of falling apart, and even an anticipatory dread of losing consciousness. Bring this panic under control, though, and reasonable amounts of anxiety can then fan the flames of life and vitality. It can be the flint that fires a creative spirit.

In just a few minutes, we finished packing the car, evacuated, and became refugees. We've all seen vivid TV images of people fleeing disaster, oppression, and war, but those images are devoid of the smell of smoke, the thrust of whipping wind, the tension of immediate danger, the intensity of a fire out of control, the urgency of taking action.

Although TV is more immediate and "on the scene" than newspapers, it still lacks the taste of real experience. Images and stories change so quickly that to feel sadness, joy, empathy, or concern is almost impossible. And without those emotions, the see-er remains separate from the seen. Watch enough TV news and life becomes a collage of changing stories, of individual frames of a film seen piecemeal and out of context, empty of perspective, soul, and any connection to what we are seeing. We sit there numb to the pain and suffering on the screen but also ripe for depression, anxiety, restlessness, unbridled anger, obsessions, addictions, troublesome relationships, and feeling that nothing means much of anything. In philosopher Martin

Buber's terminology, TV replaces the primary I-Thou relationship with I-It, which leads to alienation and anomie.

As I stood next to the car just before we drove away, I felt exposed. The fire was burning away my defenses and revealing part of my core that I'd been running away from for years. The forest had always offered me an escape route whenever I got too close to the shadows inside me, a refuge where I could release the pressure and add light to the dim mix. Now, all that remained were smoke-and-mirror memories, and the urgent need to run. I was face to face with fear, and quickly in the car and in flight.

We drove out of the smoke and paused to look back at the inferno on the ridge that appeared, in the dark, like a solar storm raging on the sun. A part of me was burning, and I cried. I cried as I watched the park burn. I cried for the animals scattering in panic. I cried for the trees. I cried for the residents of the ridge who would never again feel quite safe in the quiet of an autumn Sunday afternoon. The forest was burning, dying, and, at that moment, it looked as if nothing could stop those dragons of flame from consuming everything for miles.

At times like this, we want to cry out, ask why, even blame and berate God for allowing such destruction and hardship. But that only diverts us from the pain and fear that disasters call up in us, because all catastrophes mirror our mortality. They challenge us to consider not how much we have accumulated but how we handle our emotions and how much faith we have in ourselves, in our community, in something greater than ourselves. Catastrophes destroy our brittle perceptions and images of how the world is and will be.

Disasters ache with endings—abrupt and unplanned—and Westerners, for the most part, are not prepared to deal with them. Instead we live with blinders and earplugs and headsets on high volume as we take care of business in the present and perhaps a few hours into the future. We live in a fairy tale where everything is scripted to work out in the end. When disaster comes, rather than looking at ourselves honestly and directly so we learn how we handle loss and disappointment, we avoid the work of self-discovery and scan the horizon for something external that will divert our attention from examining, and ultimately enjoying, our inner life. We see the disaster, register its destruction and the effect it has on our lives, and then deflect, repress, deny, forget, and bury it deep down in our consciousness. It's too painful, too overwhelming, so we keep our feelings at bay with our vast arsenal of technology, from the Internet to mindless sitcoms to violent video games to Jerry Springer TV to 500-channel satellite systems to the evening news and loud commercials.

It's only when disaster strikes close to home and heart, when it involves someone or something we love deeply, that we band together to help our neighbors. When disaster is right up in our face, we can no longer run and hide or blame it on fate, karma, Mother Nature, or God. It's then that people roll up their sleeves and pitch in.

~

The park was closed for a long time after the fire. With no access to Sky Trail, or to any other trail, I was without an important sacred space where I could take my grief over this burned land and Lorraine's departure. I was wounded, and the trail was wounded, and I could not walk it and soothe those wounds, or my own.

Some months later, the Park Service began offering guided van tours through the area, apparently so that the local residents could see the devastation firsthand and begin whatever grieving they needed to do. It was one of the most sensitive things I'd ever seen a government agency do. The mood was somber as we drove through the heart of the burn down Limantour Road. The slow ride felt like a funeral procession. Most of us were strangers to one another, but we became linked by a common grief and shock that left us too stunned to speak. Some looked out the window in disbelief. Some looked down, seemingly in prayer...or tears. One woman I knew looked around and caught my eye. As at a funeral, we were both comforted somehow by each other's presence. The blackened forest was still smoldering and smoking even though several weeks had passed. We could see the ocean where it had previously been hidden by trees. I felt as if I were in a war zone. No birds. No wildlife. Only the wind broke the silence. As we passed Sky Trail, I glanced around anxiously, fearing for favorite trees, animals, and, of course, the huckleberries. The woman ranger who was guiding the tour reminded us that fire is necessary for the health of the forest, a natural part of the cycle of growth and plant propagation. Because the area had not burned in more than 50 years, the forest floor had been like a massive tinderbox waiting to be ignited. "All it needed," she continued, in the tone of a compassionate technician slightly more comfortable with facts than feelings, "was heat, dryness, wind, and a bit of human error—all happening at about the same time."

EXPLORING YOUR PATH

> Take a few minutes to think about what makes you anxious. How does anxiety manifest in your body? Sweaty palms? A pounding heart? Lightheadedness? How do you manage it? Is it ever a motivating force that pushes you forward?

> What would you take with you if your house or apartment was threatened with fire and you had only 20 minutes to get out—and no chance to make a second trip? Make a list. You may want to repeat this exercise from time to time as your possessions and circumstances change.

> Have you ever been an eyewitness to destruction caused by fire, storm, or flood? Spend a few minutes reflecting on or writing about that experience. Put yourself in the place of the victims. Try to feel what they must have been feeling. Increasing your sensitivity to others will heighten your intimacy with all things that make up this universe. On a daily basis, it will also change the way you watch and respond to the evening news.

Loving and Grieving a Tree

How intimacy with a tree begins, I am not certain. But I have always found myself more comfortable around some familiar trees, as if we were related, as if my blood and their sap were flowing at the same pace in the same plane of consciousness. Describing all the objective ways we can relate to and perceive a tree, Martin Buber wrote in his classic *I and Thou,* "It can, however, also come about, if I have both will and grace, that in considering the tree I become bound up in relation to it. The tree is now no longer It. I have been seized by the power of exclusiveness." The concepts "tree" and "I" disappear. The spirit of the tree and the spirit within me are the same.

I have felt this intimacy with several trees. One was an old pine in the forest near my cabin in New Hampshire. This wise grandmother, thick in girth and handsome in shape, had birthed many of the young pines that sprouted about. Another was a tall, lanky, straggling tree that towered over the cabin. It had just a tuft of branches near its top, which made botanical identification difficult, but I called it Ol' Herc, and it provided comfort and companionship throughout the sometimes harsh seasons and lonesome days. A battered loner, it stood out among the others and felt to me like a friendly neighbor, always there with support and a willingness to listen to my kvetching. When I met the second largest tree in the world, Big Buck, which has been standing magnificent in stature and age in a forest south of Yosemite since before the birth of Jesus, it did not speak or listen to me in the tree whispers that intimacy requires.

Many handsome trees—Douglas firs and Pacific madrone and California laurel and an occasional California live oak—grace Sky Trail, but only one ever called to me in ways that led to intimacy. I never named it but it had character, that tree. It was the Bishop pine—the only one of its species on that part of the trail—that rose, nicely crowned and standing separate from other trees, just off the trailhead. Maybe it was the simultaneity of that standing apart from while being a part of the whole that bound our characters together. In any case, what resulted was camaraderie—a connection that deepened over time into a core feeling that I experienced as intimacy.

Time and attention. Perhaps these, along with the mysteries of attraction, are among the essentials that lead to love and intimacy. Still, something more, something unknown, ancient, and primeval existed between that Bishop pine and me. Perhaps I had once been a tree myself, and that pine a person who had sat under me and written me poems full of endearments and gratitude. In olden days, trees were certainly held more sacred than today. They were noticed and blessed, acknowledged as part of life rather than just props in the background. We were linked, that tree and I, in a bond that had been created well before the supposed Big Bang beginning. I could not understand it intellectually, but I knew that before the before the before, that tree and I had embraced in eternal love.

~

Thwarted by changing winds, increased humidity, and 2,000 firefighters from all over the state, the wildfire only brushed Sky Trail. Few trees died, but all it takes is one ember in tall, dry grass to burn a tree at the stake. And that is what happened to the Bishop pine.

When I finally saw it, weeks after the fire, it still looked alive, though blackened, with tufts of green needles near its crown, and I prayed each time I walked past that it would survive. I had seen other trees come back from supposedly deadly burns. I refused to believe that it was dead. But eventually I could not deny it. My old friend was gone.

Dead.

What in the world is dead, my intellectual, rational self asked? I had dealt with death before—my grandmother, a favorite aunt, a boyhood best friend, my ex-wife, my father. But it still threw me. Did it mean gone forever? Was it something other than alive? How did being dead affect my relationship with the dead? With those I had loved and lost? Was I not still best friends with my childhood best friend, Manny Fein, who died in a car crash shortly after graduation from high school? Was I not still in relationship with my ex-wife Donna, who committed suicide soon after we divorced? As Stephen Levine, the spiritual teacher and writer on death and dying, asked in his book of the same title, "Who dies?" Does anything die? Can matter be destroyed? Can it be created? Or does it just change form? Do all living things return to God? Or to love? Or to nature? Or just to dust? Who is the who within the who? And is there a form, beyond the physical plane, where the dead still live? The answers to these questions move into the realm of belief, a realm that my Zen training reacts against. One of my early teachers, the Korean Zen Master Seung Sahn, based his teachings on the instructions, "Don't know!" and "Always go straight ahead." "When you die, just die," he would have said. "No thinking." And my Zen head finds comfort and wisdom in that: a teaching of No Teaching. Nothing to cling to. Nothing to separate me from the experience. Nothing to launch me into the future, where I and almost everyone spend much too much time.

But my Jewish heart, that untidy place that insists on remaining in the realm of beliefs, knows something that my Zen head misses. I can't quite put my finger on it yet, but it has to do with my Bubbe, my grandmother, and her blintzes, and Zeyde, my grandfather, and his thick hands holding me on his lap, and my father cracking jokes until I was rolling on the floor, and Donna's lovely smile and contagious laugh, and Manny asking my mother if she could take us to City Hall so he and I could become blood brothers. On some deep level of existence that my Western mind pays little attention to, all of these are alive and with me every time I conjure up their memory.

~

And so to with my old friend the Bishop pine. Slowly, a black blood sucked the life out of each limb, twig, and needle, making the old pine vulnerable to the coastal winds, until one day a winter storm wrestled it down. I came upon it lying on its side with roots exposed, grotesque, and tangled.

But as I walked beside it, attending to it and whispering words of love and gratitude, I still saw it in its original shape. Sentimental? Too precious for these steely times? Maybe, but a beloved friend was lying there, and wouldn't I have acknowledged any dead friend or close relative that way? Was I any less related to the Bishop pine than I was to my closest human friends or relatives?

Nearby, I saw small saplings, little pines born of this fallen parent. They were straight and supple, bending like willows, branches and needles tossed in all directions by the wind but going nowhere. The great gnarled trunk of the old pine was already rotting. Chunks of bark had flaked off in the first phases of decomposition. It was spring, and the earth was green with shoots of wild grains and grasses, lupine and blue-eyed grass, yarrow and clover.

Dead.

The sound of the word slaps hard, then breaks off like a dog's single bark at 3 A.M. Was the old pine really dead? I was grieving for it, but had our intimacy also died now that its form had changed? What had changed? The tree was still there but in another form. And even now that it has rotted away completely, I still remember it, as I do my loving grandmother 40 years after her death.

Death and life forever play hide-and-seek with us as they create a Great Illusion that something just seen is now gone. Life, as the old pine and its offspring proved, is continuous and eternal. Where only one tree grew before, a new grove of Bishop pines is taking root.

~

Tree man that I am, I sometimes imagine myself being a tree, as I suspect snake people try to picture themselves crawling and devouring fat rodents, and birders flying to a nest and feeding fledglings. I find it easy to visualize being permanently rooted to the same spot, growing, breathing, swaying, feeling songbirds or raptors perching upon me as a fly might alight on my nose during sitting meditation, sensing a bobcat or a human passing by, bracing myself against a Pacific storm, healing after losing a limb or being seared by fire, holding fast against stiff spring winds and soothed by the first baby-blue forget-me-nots and wild purple irises. It might be boring at times, and I might wish I were elsewhere, wish I were something other than a tree, but a tree must put those thoughts aside and accept its tree-life.

Still, if my human life is any indication, I think I would have a hard time, if it came right down to it, being a tree. I would be restless, always leaning this way or that. I would be critical of myself for not being enough of a tree, and perhaps critical of others for peeing on me or carving initials in my bark. I would despair at having what I thought was no control over my life. I would grow anxious with nothing to do, nowhere to go, with having to content myself with a lifetime of tree-ing.

Then again, with life distilled to its simplest and noblest terms, I might be a happier tree than I imagine. If I were tree-ing in a protected wilderness like Point Reyes, I might enjoy the silence. Except for the occasional discordant human voice, distant chainsaw, or raucous crow's caw, silence reigns. Things grow and things are eaten, things die and things decay, all without much commotion. The sun glides through the sky soundlessly, as do the moon, planets, clouds, and stars. And though the wind blows hard and destructively at times, it does so as a jazz saxophonist might delve into harmonic dissonance—it may be unsettling at times, but it's still music.

Even now, whenever I pass this old, fallen friend, I feel a kinship that comes with intimacy. Others pass and take no notice of it. A passing glance tells them that it is dead, and, as such, useless and no longer worthy of attention.

But in the woods death and life are inseparable and complementary. One leads to the other leads to the other, and neither comes first. Did death exist before the beginning? How could life start if matter cannot be created? Science can't answer this, nor can religion. It's too much a process for religious dogma to explain. The more I walk the trail and wander the forest, the less I realize I know about any absolute beginnings or absolute ends. Nature simply creates, cares for, and accepts or adapts to what is. Yes, the Bishop pine is dead. I do not deny that, but can anyone say that it is no longer part of the forest? Are its charred remains any less essential for the growth of the forest than the harrier hawk that keeps the rodent population in check? I will never again see the pine's unique form again, reaching in all directions, filling the sky with needles and cones, providing support to songbirds and owls, giving shade to bobcats and beetles. That saddens me. I am a human being, and humans grieve for the loss of what we love. But I am also more than a human being. I am fuller, part of an infinite universe that defies definition or categorization.

I know that because when I look at that tree now, I feel love, which is to say that I feel no separation between the tree and me. Zen students spend tough, cross-legged hours on the cushion enduring physical and emotional pain to accomplish something that is already, on deep psychic levels, true—that experience of complete unity with all forms of life. Can such love be sought after? Can the thinking mind, trained to learn, plan, rationalize, and produce, give itself up and commune with something other than itself? The very nature of mind is to seek, to desire. Chasing intimacy is like trying to grab hold of a handful of water with one hand. "The Thou meets me through grace," to quote Buber again, this time on the primary divine force that embraces all life, "it is not found by seeking...The Thou meets me. But I step into direct relation with it...All real living is meeting."

My relationship with the Bishop pine had nothing to do with my thinking mind, or with knowing its botanical name or its processes of photosynthesis, nothing to do with photographs or prose or poetry, or any other concept. My relationship had to do with love—not romantic I-can't-live-without-you love, or follow-your-bliss-hug-and-kiss love, or love-thy-neighbor dogmatic-religious love, but the love you can feel without needing a word to describe or sanctify it. Such love dwells in everyday things: a kitten dashes to the door to greet me; a wildflower holds its ground against a strong wind; the warm, open smile of a kindred spirit greets me on the trail; a sparrow hawk perches at the top of a tall fir and preens its wings; a thousand ants work a two-foot plot of land in communion and community; a great horned owl calls to its mate; a young neighbor child, filled with innocence and trust, calls my name.

When love is present, God is present. In that moment, the neighbor child is God saying, "I see you. I like you. Listen to me. Come and talk with me." It takes awareness, an appreciation of small matters and of their true essence, to transform the mundane into the miracles they actually are. We seek out gurus, read self-help books, attend religious services, and go on lengthy retreats to find our truth and how to live this truth. But the answers lie before us in nature every moment of every day. Answers are revealed every time we give or receive love—not codified in a catechism but discovered anew each time like a parable.

Answers to important life questions cannot be pigeonholed into basic principles or 10 easy steps or so many inviolable laws or truths. Answers are not frozen in perpetuity. Answers flow, blow, fog out, flood, and get caked in mud. What answers does my dead tree friend give me? That death is good? That decay grows? That fire is good, so everything should eventually burn? That everything alive finally dies? No, it gives no direct answers. Where we are as a species, living far beneath our emotional, mental, physical, and spiritual capacities, is the result of our efforts to permanently carve the laws of inner and outer nature in stone, to take what is organic and elegant and to imprison it in dogma and theorems.

Has the Cyber-Information Age brought us closer to the truth of ourselves and our relationship with all things living, dead, animate, or inanimate? Has our cataloguing and categorizing and naming and experimenting and studying nature helped us to understand our own nature—that *sine qua non* of understanding everything? Have we any true wisdom to offer our children, our future generations, or ourselves? Can we put aside naming just for a moment and come into complete relationship with the universe?

Naming the Bishop pine describes it, but love does not arise from the naming. In fact, naming often results in a proprietary relationship, another "notch" on the namer's list of objects possessed.

When Julia Butterfly Hill perched atop a thousand-year-old coast redwood, she did so not to study it but, in an act of civil disobedience and divine obedience, to save it. Those who "own" the redwoods in northern California may have developed "integrated forest management," but they have no Tree Wisdom to pass on. Instead, they have dutifully named and classified and mapped, consigning trees to so many board feet or fence posts or pieces of garden furniture, forgetting that nature grew trees in the garden well before humans arrived.

Julia simply loved redwoods, and, as a result of that love, followed a higher law and occupied a tree that science calls *Sequoia sempervirens*, and she called "Luna." God in the guise of a 24-year-old woman sat atop another divine manifestation and told us that Luna was part of our collective family and that we must love and care for all its members. Anytime we remember our eternal fabric, God abides in some form or another. Julia expressed this connection in a poem she wrote after the Pacific Lumber Company clear-cut a section of trees near Luna. While the shaken tree held her, she could sense it was beginning to weep tears of sap, as if mourning the desecration. At that moment, she penned these words:

OFFERINGS TO LUNA

A tree
a life so many years gone by
history bound in each new
ring and every scar
I lay nestled in Her arms
I listen to all She has to say
She speaks to me through my
bare feet...my hands
She speaks to me on the
wind...and in the rain
telling me stories born long
before my time
Wisdom
as only Ancient Elders know
Truths
passed to me through
Nature's perfect lips
She cries
Her overwhelming grief
sap that clings to me...
to my soul
I wrap my arms around Her
offering the only solace
That I know
giving myself as the only gift
I have to give
a pitiful offering
to a Goddess such as this
but of myself
it is all that I have to give

Julia transformed her love of redwoods into environmental and political action that got the attention of people like me who would never go to such extremes but who would act in our own impassioned way if educated and inspired enough. Her action, spawned from love, inspired me to write about the Bishop pine that I had come to know and love, and I hope that I in turn will inspire others to consider what in nature they love and how they might act to preserve what is left. According to Dave Foreman, the founder of Earth First! and the author of *The Big Outside*, two million acres of wilderness fall to development every year. Although nature is still creating new land and wilderness via earthquakes and volcanic activity, it is doing so at a slower pace than we're destroying it. What do you love? What will you do to save what remains?

~

The Bishop pine lies on its side like a huge reclining Buddha awaiting Parinirvana, his final journey of no return toward deep abiding calm. After years of upright service, in death the pine still serves the land and the living. In the Jewish faith, the spirit of the dead is kept alive by remembering, by piecing back together all the characteristics of a person that are seemingly scattered by death. At their core, all breathing things are but spirit—indeed, the holistic physician Andrew Weil points out that in many languages the words for "breath" and "spirit" are the same—wrapped for a relatively brief time in our clay garments, as the American spiritual sojourner and teacher Peace Pilgrim called the body. Whenever I remember my Bubbe, I again feel awash in her love and caring, and grateful that she passed them on to me and the rest of our family. The Bishop pine shows me that as well, for all around it I see the legacy of life that results from love—through its seed, the tree lives on, growing the forest.

By acknowledging and loving the Bishop pine (though it could be any tree or plant), I meld with its spirit and ensure my own place in eternity. Love fills the black holes, Stephen Hawking, and love is where we all return—trees, butterflies, skunks, rats, people from the most pious saints to the vilest of villains, petunias, pythons, and my old, lap-loving cat who died last year. Love receives us all, love chews us up and gently spits us out again and again until we finally understand and remember from whence we came and finally etch love into the foreground of our lives...as that Bishop pine did.

Knowing this changes everything. Whenever I've lived a moment of love, I've never been afraid in that moment. On the contrary, I've always felt fully alive and fully in touch with life. If death and love are inseparable, one flowing from the other, then in life we have the opportunity to love deeply and, in so doing, to approach death without fear. Death stops being a vast, frightening unknown. If love is the original material of the universe—and if you've ever truly felt love, you know this to be true—what is there to fear in returning to it? In death we will be enveloped by love.

EXPLORING YOUR PATH

> Take a few minutes with your journal to list at least 10 things in nature that you love.

> Take each of the top five items on your list and write a short poem that describes your observations, feelings, and impressions of each one.

> Have you ever loved and lost something in nature? Take some time to reflect on this and, when you are ready, spend 10 minutes writing about it. What did the love feel like? And the loss? Was your lost love local, regional, national, or international?

> If you've lost loved ones—family, friends, pets—how do you remember them? With prayers, rituals, altars, photographs?   Spend a few minutes writing about your ways of grieving and remembrance.

Taproots

"There will be a sense of the flow of life—that you are brought into new vistas as you surrender to moving with the flow of God," Julia Cameron, in *The Artist's Way*, writes. On the trail, that flow was always available, and I went there often after the park reopened seeking to heal my wounds of loss from the fire and from Lorraine's leaving.

Because the trail too was wounded, its counsel was even more profound and relevant. It could help heal me, and I could help heal it, merely by the way I perceived it. That we can change something or someone by how we consider it is not a new concept. In my experience with the mentally disabled, people made faster and more solid recoveries if the rapport and trust between us was strong. The simplest gesture of goodwill— a welcoming look or a good word—made them feel noticed, respected, and honored, as long as those gestures were genuine and not consciously chosen therapeutic techniques.

We all know from our own experience how much a warm smile can bring us hope and brighten a dark day. For those suffering from mental disabilities, one day of darkness and hopelessness could result in a desperate dive off a bridge, which happened all too often. We know that human babies, monkeys, and even newborn rats respond to loving touches with enhanced growth and development—and to neglect with emotional and physical atrophy, and even death. In the animal world, we've all seen the cringing or aggressive behaviors of dogs that have been abused or neglected, compared to the happy, trusting behaviors of dogs that have been lavished with love. In my own first marriage, I learned that a relationship could change in an instant from sweet to sour, from loving and affirming to suspicious and hostile, by a wisp of a thought or the lash of a disparaging word. Even worse, many of us are so unloving and critical of ourselves on a daily basis that we cause ourselves great mental confusion and suffering.

"What drives someone crazy?" wrote Gangaji, the American-born female spiritual teacher in the lineage of Indian sage Sri Ramana Maharshi, in *You Are That*. "It seems like, from the studies of early childhood, it is some profound lack of nurturance, some profound lack of recognition of the true spiritual being that one is." And it doesn't take much negativity to do that damage, she added: "If you are sensitive, even if it is not grossly profound, it is experienced as profound."

Even the plant world is sensitive to love and hate. All of us who garden know how sensitive seedlings are and how they respond to a loving touch or thought, but now research has confirmed what psychics and mystics have known for centuries—that plants sense and feel. Scientists have found that they can alter botanical experiments by how they look at or think about plants. One study demonstrated that the needle of a kind of galvanic skin response device jumped when a researcher was about to cut a plant's stem. And when I, a tree man, pat a tree, a 2000-year-old redwood, for example, I know that it senses my loving attitude through the intelligence of its cells. Every fiber of bark, trunk, branch, needle, and seed is like a thread in a web that telegraphs the intent of my touch.

Love heals. Most anything else, including indifference, harms. That's why Sky Trail was a place of healing for my soul, a wild place that felt as comfortable as an old summer retreat returned to year after year. It was a place where the roots of love, nurtured within, could find a rich soil in which to sprout.

~

For me, those roots were tended and nurtured early on, mostly by my Bubbe. She was short and stout and buxom with fleshy arms that liked to hug and a smile that could melt the cruelest tyrant. My mother always said she was quite anxious and high-strung, but my adoring eyes saw none of that. Nor did I feel any negativity in her thinking or actions. Her roots were poor, her parents peasant-farmer Russian Jews. I remember little of what she used to say, but my memory and all my senses remain saturated with the clinking and tinkering of her cooking, with the sight of plates piled high with traditional Ashkenazi Jewish foods whose blend of consonants evoked their taste, texture, and volume: kreplach, blintzes, lokshen kugel, kasha, fried matzos, latkes, borscht, hamantaschen, challah, knishes, rugelach, kishkeh, and kasheh varnishkes. If our family were somehow of Mexican-Jewish roots and I had died, these would be the foods that would entice me to return on the Day of the Dead – that first day of November when the favorite foods of deceased family members are placed on an altar and the departed are invited back to share the feast with the living. Considering this tradition, I do on occasion eat an old favorite with my grandmother in mind.

On some occasions, such as the meal after the fast of Yom Kippur, the day of atonement and the holiest Jewish holiday, Bubbe would spend the whole day cooking. She would bring out plates—elegant and old and etched, piled high with cheese blintzes and kreplach and lots of sour cream. At the center of the table stood one of our family heirlooms—the antique porcelain Chinese Laughing Buddha that I took with me when I fled the Point Reyes fire. Bare-chested, big-bellied, surrounded by adoring bodhisattvas dressed in brocaded robes, this Buddha wore a little red yarmulke that Bubbe had knitted to cover his bald pate.

At these feasts, my mother, of course, helped with the cooking and serving, my father kibitzed and joked, and my brother Hank and I ate and ate and ate. My Zeyde, a baker by trade, and kind and loving in his own quiet way, ate silently and soon retired to his chair in the living room to continue reading the Jewish newspaper. Sometimes relatives would be there, too, or a neighbor, and, at some point during the evening, a young man we all called Crazy Gilbert would peep in our front window to observe the goings-on. Today we would label him paranoid schizophrenic, control his symptoms and his personality with medications, and keep him as far away from our front windows as possible, but for us he was an accepted member of our community. He was familiar and we all knew from experience that his curiosity about us was harmless. Whenever we saw him, we would always wave to him, and he would wave back and continue his rounds. Perhaps Crazy Gilbert helped me, later in my work with the severely mentally ill, to honor them as people rather than just seeing, and fearing, them as walking diagnoses.

In 1950, when I was four, my father, after years of just getting by through the Great Depression and World War II, was making big money with a government-subsidized school that taught the building trades to returning GIs. Until then, we had lived three generations in one house, surrounded by a stable and familiar neighborhood. With our new affluence, we migrated from South Philadelphia's Jewish ghetto, where everyone knew everyone, to Wynnefield's Jewish suburbs, where hardly anyone, except we kids, met or knew anyone. Bubbe and Zeyde stayed put, comfortable in the row house they owned and surrounded by all that was familiar and safe—other relatives, old friends, and the orthodox synagogue on the corner of 8th and Porter. They were, of course, sad to see us go. In their ways, families stayed together no matter what the conditions. My mother and Bubbe were particularly close, and tears flowed at the thought of separating. I was four and I can still remember the sadness permeating the house. But ultimately, everyone accepted the changing times and the need to advance economically and socially. My grandparents, happy to see my parents achieving some financial success, gave us their blessings. However, the loss of connection with our roots in South Philly created the first cracks in our familial foundation of love and opened an era of estrangement.

In 1955, Bubbe suffered a stroke at my cousin Richard's bar mitzvah. When I saw her lying there on the floor surrounded by panicky relatives, I felt faint—a 10-year-old watching love itself fall. My aunt Fritzi took me aside and consoled me, which

I have always remembered and loved her for. Three days later, Bubbe, our family matriarch, our spiritual and emotional pillar, died. Zeyde hadn't gone to the party. He didn't like my cousin's grandparents, who were also my grandparents on my father's side. They were wealthier people who had come over from pre-Hitler Germany on a luxury liner, and he felt they had always looked down on him because he was only a bagel baker from a small town near Kiev. Although Bubbe had urged him to attend, he had insisted that he didn't feel well. But he never got over the guilt of having not gone because he felt that his refusal had upset her and triggered her stroke. Soon after the funeral, he moved into our suburban home. For him, it was like finding himself living on a strange planet. He would sit by the window each day looking out at nothing, feeling nothing, wanting nothing except his wife back. Although he was a relatively healthy man, he died six months later, "of a broken heart," as everyone said.

I think we all felt guilty as well—for having let the family closeness fall apart, for having left her behind in South Philly. I remembered that she had cooked a huge meal—plate after plate of kreplach—the night before her stroke, and, in my 10-year-old mind, I thought that she had literally cooked her heart out.

After her death, our family crumbled. My mother, with her mother gone, retreated into a self-absorbed and self-indulgent world. She became morose and completely unavailable emotionally, and spent more and more time out—shopping, lunching, playing mah-jongg. One afternoon when my father was away on business, she failed to come home for dinner. Hank, who was six years older, and I became frightened. We perched on the couch like owls and peered through the drapes as we scanned the dark street for any sign of her car. We both feared that she was dead, though neither of us could speak of or even hint at the possibility. We both got so tense that he eventually accused me of having stinking breath and ordered me upstairs to brush my teeth. While I was in the bathroom, she came back, but she scarcely seemed aware of the anxiety she had caused us. Meanwhile, my father's business fell victim to a feud with a partner, my mother's brother, Sam. In fact, family feuds began breaking out more and more often.

When love is lost, simple words can divide a family. In ours, the buffer of forgiveness—that ability to forget and move on and understand that people are only human—collapsed with Bubbe's death. When our family was united in love, when we lived closer to the elders, we remembered more who we were as Jews, where we had come from, and how we had helped one another in the face of tyranny and oppression. When that love died, misunderstandings arising out of greed multiplied and often resulted in feuds—not momentary outbursts that soon ended, but smoldering, festering vendettas that could, and often did, last a lifetime. Relatives, business partners, friends were cast out and ignored as if they had never lived. I lost several uncles, aunts, and cousins as a result. Many years later, I told my mother that our family's penchant for feuding had always troubled me. "You just don't want anyone getting angry at anyone else," she countered.

"No, I don't have a problem with people getting angry," I answered. "But when people get angry in this family, they stop talking to one another for the rest of their lives."

My words had hit a raw nerve and triggered repressed feelings that surfaced when words approached the depth of pain we all felt around the feuding. Love defined our heritage and we were all grieving its loss. I know I was.

That we, as Jews, should have been feuding with one another after all we had been through was a paradox. I had never heard of any feuding in my family, at least on the Russian side, before we arrived in America. My grandparents came from Winnitzer, a small village near Kiev, and it was the Winnitzer Association, made up of former neighbors from the town who had settled in Philadelphia, that helped them to get established. For years, the group would meet each month to sing Yiddish songs, reminisce, and share a potluck meal that offered them the same kind of community and solidarity they had experienced in Russia. Zeyde baked at night and so couldn't attend, but, during hard times he gave away huge quantities of his bagels and challah to hungry families he had known in Russia and who had helped him when he had first arrived—alone, for, like many Russian-Jewish men, he came over first, got established, and then sent money for Bubbe and the children to join him later. At the beginning of the 20th century, young Russian Jews, like him, were escaping conscription to fight senseless wars that meant certain death for those on the front lines.

That support and community was my heritage, but when the feeling of family and community dissipated in anger, feuding, and alienation, I drifted away, disheartened. Perhaps I should have stayed, but even after 40 years away, I still link anger and even love with loss, estrangement, and irreconcilable differences. Although my parents loved and cared for me, the solid foundation of love that had absorbed and transformed anger died with my Russian grandparents, and I carried my melancholy for many years. Like my mother, I failed to fully accept Bubbe's death, and I abandoned my family, essentially, so I wouldn't have to face the sadness that they and their feuding represented. For I saw in the eyes of all of them the spirit of Bubbe—unrealized, unfulfilled, unknown. I left to begin a search for that lost Grail of love—and the person I had been would never return.

~

That search has been an active one, involving marriage, divorce, meditation, therapy, living in different places, trying different jobs, always hoping to rekindle the deep, loving roots and community my grandparents represented. At each way station, I found elements of their legacy and stored them in my soul's backpack. At each way station, I also rediscovered a bit more of my Bubbe within me. And when I eventually arrived at Point Reyes, and experienced the nurturing ways of the park, I was ready to settle in and be more at ease. The fire was a test of my capacity to again deal with the death of something I loved.

When the park reopened and I reentered the trail, it still smelled acrid from the wildfire, and the scorched trees looked like wounded and dead soldiers on a battlefield. But the trail had escaped the devastation wreaked elsewhere because bulldozers had muscled it wider in places and created access for fire equipment. The firefighters had waged fierce battles to the north and kept the flames from engulfing Sky Trail. Some trees—including my Bishop pine—and brush had burned, but the damage had been minimal compared to the holocaust just a mile or so north and west to the ocean. In fact, it was only the ocean that had stopped it in that direction.

The fire and the fight to contain it had been honest, brutal, and direct, without the innuendo that often plagues human relations. The bruised, blackened forest, changed though it now was, was also adapting and shifting to create the right conditions so growth could continue. Nature had begun recovering and adjusting immediately. Though forms had changed, the interconnections of species remained intact.

Sky Trail, as my feet bore witness, truly was a living thing in its own right, awake to the core, and the obvious recipient of that unbroken chain of care. As I contemplated its origins and its present state, I began to place my own origins and my present condition into an evolutionary context. I was alone, divorced, relatively poor, with no children and no property, but I had a long-term love affair with this wilderness trail. Regret—that emotional acid that so corrodes the joys of the present—receded and my mind began to catch up with what my feet already knew of the ground—that instead of denying or lamenting difficult changes when they arise, it's best to face and respond to them. My task was not to subdue negative thoughts, emotions, and desires, but to look at them, experience them, and make wise decisions around expressing them. The thinking mind was not an enemy—as the Buddhist view is often misinterpreted— but a part of oneself that needed closer attention, understanding, and integration with spirit, heart, and hand. Like Narcissus, the Western mind became enchanted with the illusion of its separateness and its ability to analyze and label, eventually digressing into self-absorption ("says I to myself says I," as Alan Watts put it). Ending this illusion, which once seen can be smashed instantly, dissolves self-centeredness and returns the dissident fragments to a whole. In South Philadelphia, surrounded by the love of family and community, I had seen something of this, and now, on and around this wilderness trail, I saw it again. When all parts merged, a sense of place emerged—that which was both under foot and within the heart.

EXPLORING YOUR PATH

> Who loved you when you were a child? Reflect and record your childhood memories of love in your journal.

> Go to your favorite nearby place in nature. Note your mood when you enter, and any specific feelings you experience. Settle yourself down and spend some time there. Has anything changed? Your mood? Emotions? Thoughts? How do you perceive the landscape? Did any life questions arise? Answers?

> Today, pay attention to expressions of love that you receive and give. Keep track of loving thoughts that you don't express, and of negative, critical thoughts as well. During the coming week, take a few minutes each day to inventory these expressions and thoughts in your journal. At the end of the week, look over what you've written and see if any insights arise.

Stalking Silence

Love blossoms when thinking quiets and living begins. I stop and gaze at the magnificence of a Douglas fir cone bending with humility, enfolding itself like a monk in robes, bobbing in the afternoon springtime breeze, hanging in the momentary hush of the early evening air, made still by the chill just after sunset. The manuals call the cone's shape "pendulous," a word I like very much. I imagine for a moment being "pendulous," hanging freely, swaying, swinging, dancing through the day, tossed in storms but riding them out with dignity, courage, and faith.

If I were pendulous, perhaps I would not worry so much about the morrow. I would not resist the action of life—free, trusting, wild. I would not change positions as much and would stay in place more to face shadows and meet fear head-on. For example, I once sat cross-legged for 17 hours without moving during a Buddhist meditation retreat. A zone of peace surrounded me and obviated any reason to move…buttocks settling into the sitting cushion, shoulders drifting downward to find their lowest level like water in a creek, hands resting on thighs without tension, neck and spine forming a straight though not rigid line, head as erect as a candle flame in still air, eyes shut, lips resting against each other gently, teeth and jaw suspended like stars in space. I was in pain for part of that time but saw no need to run from it. Nor did I need to pursue pleasure. For 17 hours, I hung, pendulous. For 17 hours I was simply a human being, being. But at minute 1021, I moved, opened my eyes, untwisted my legs, nodded my head, tensed my shoulders to help stretch my back, and then shattered the Grail by saying to myself, "Wow, just wait 'til the teacher hears what I've done!" Pride and pretension are the antithesis of being pendulous.

~

Surrounding each scale on the fir cone is a three-pronged bract that perhaps protects the seeds from birds and gives the cone a look of something very old and wise. The entire cone reminds me of wizened Native American shamans, each conveying life lessons by displaying a passive yet powerful vulnerability. Observing that cone, oblivious to time passing, unconcerned with the science behind its form and function or with gaining more knowledge, I rediscovered something of the Grail I had held during my 17-hour still-sit. It had to do with the quiet use of my senses, of letting my senses be pendulous, of letting them do their sensing while I hung on a tree of attention.

"A thick garment of perception is woven thread by overlapping thread," wrote Diane Ackerman in *A Natural History of the Senses*, describing the phenomenon of synesthesia, in which one sense stimulates another. As my mind emptied of any extraneous desire to do something or be somewhere else, reasons to move also vaporized, as did the need to make the moments any more complete. The rich browns of the mature cone. The silvery underbelly of fir needles sending out the sinus-opening resinous odor that prompted the Italians to call the Douglas fir *abeto odoroso*, or "fragrant fir." The neck-straining height of this, one of the world's tallest tree species, which grows at times to more than 300 feet. It is not a perfectly symmetrical tree, but at that moment I felt no need to make it, or anything else in my life, better. Without intending it to be so, without teaching me, or without my seeking its wisdom and guidance, this Douglas fir bestowed silence upon me and my busy mind and body.

Thomas Keating calls silence the language of God. He says that God appears not when bidden but when we are receptive, when we are free of even wanting God to appear. That kind of silence is not to be developed or sought after, for to do so would only add motive, and motive is already too much noise. That kind of silence has to do with grace, that noblest of states, which seems to elude most human beings but is the essence of every tree I've ever encountered. Grace means letting life emerge as it will and being present for the show. Resistance is not part of grace. Nor is regret. Nor is guilt or continual self-flagellation for "getting it wrong." In fact, as Thomas Moore asserts in *Care of the Soul*, "getting it wrong" sometimes fertilizes the soul and the grace that sprouts within it. Grace does not hurry. Nor is it impatient or frustrated by meager results. Grace can wait—lifetimes if need be.

~

There was a time in this park when one of nature's manifestations of grace, in the form of large, roaming animals, was more noticeable. Now the huge herds of elk that used to populate Inverness Ridge are gone. So are the multitudes of bears, black and grizzly. And despite the abundance of food, only a few cougars—even the wildlife managers don't know how many— still stalk the evergreen forests and coastal brush over the 200 or so square miles between Point Reyes and the Marin Headlands to the south near the Golden Gate. Bobcats are here, though. I've seen them on the trail traveling and hunting alone, sauntering along the middle of wide sections or peering out at me from the tall meadow grasses, perhaps thinking themselves invisible, like a kitten I once knew who "hid" under the bedspread, unaware that her tail and rear end were sticking out. Sighting a bobcat is a rare event, but because it has happened several times, I look forward to it and always bring binoculars. Little in this life raises my spirits like the sight of this wildcat, ever alert, with its characteristic pointy ears, more sensitive than radar, rotating and flickering and aiming and deciphering, determining in a nanosecond if the crack of a twig is benign, or threatening, or a signal that dinner has arrived.

At times I've gotten quite close. Perhaps it's been the same bobcat each time, and he has gotten used to me by now. When I spot it, I stop my walking and try stalking, a form of motion that has much more to do with duration than with endurance. It takes time to stalk a wild animal, particularly a bobcat, which is usually the stalker. The key is silence, taking each step deliberately, as if crossing a minefield, being careful not to contact crackly things like leaves, twigs, or branches hidden under brush. Any sound outside of the ordinary forest peeps, chirps, whistles, and crackles will send a bobcat running, and a bobcat running is a bobcat quickly out of sight.

Cats wild and domestic respond favorably to silence and to movement that does not disturb the normal noises in the woods. So with stalking, I must acknowledge the language of God with my every movement. And the more silent I become in body, mind, and spirit, the more unified I can become with that wild, grace-full cat.

When the stalking is good—and I'm talking about one single step—everything gels. Mind quiets, sight sees all, skin feels the wind and its direction, nose smells scents and where they blow in relation to the cat, ears hear the sounds of movement, brain analyzes all the data efficiently and instantly sends the necessary signals to limbs and organs and glands. I make no sound as I move from bush to tree to open ground. On that open ground, when I become visible to the cat, I know if the stalking has stopped being something I am consciously doing and has become simply who I am at that moment. I can see it in the bobcat's eyes, for when they look back at me without fear, he and I are in the same sacred space, like two planets lined up beneath the moon. We are at ease with each other. Then, inevitably, I step on a twig or rattle the keys in my pocket or cough or think about something unrelated to this vast moment. The spell of sanctity shatters. The bobcat disappears like an apparition, leaving me standing knee-high in a grassy meadow and covered in the mess my mind has made.

No doubt the Miwoks were more accomplished stalkers than I. In their day, elk and antelope grazed the native bunchgrasses that covered these hills. But when the Spaniards imported cows to feast on the abundant meadows, they also imported, caught in the hooves of those beasts, annual European grass seed that took hold and choked and bullied the native species into fewer and smaller corners. With the bunchgrasses decimated, the elk and antelope lost a perennial dietary staple and, within about a hundred years were gone as well, after eons of living on the ridge.

When I stalk the bobcat, I see the elk and bear and antelope of old. I see the bunchgrasses and the ocean-to-ridge displays of wildflower orange, deep blue, red, green, purple, white, and sky-blue with their fanciful names—iris, poppy, blue-eyed grass, Indian paintbrush, larkspur, star tulip, clover, lupine, tidy tips, and phacelia. I see the skies black with migratory ducks and geese. I see the Miwok people, living not a "lifestyle," as we say today, but a life, full of sharing, providing, playing, and honoring. Even today, their descendants yell "Ho!" after each ritual and prayer at their annual Big Time gathering, when the native peoples come together to renew bonds with each other and the land in a meadow and reconstructed village near the park's headquarters. The tribes today are much smaller in number, but to hear them shout with one voice is to realize a greeting to all life everywhere.

In this grassy, flowered meadow just off Sky Trail, purple with tall tree lupine, man and wild mammal, with Mother Nature as witness and mediator, face off in an ancient dance that Western peoples have mostly forgotten. Bobcat reappears from the bush like the moon from behind a cloud, still but ready to spring away again at any sudden move from this two-legged interloper. The wildcat has seen others standing motionless, only to suddenly lunge like rattlers and attack with guns and traps.

~

As a Jew with European roots, I know something of the bob-cat's dilemma. I too have experience contradictions: trust and deception, tolerance and suspicion, hatred and violence. In one moment, conversation can be pleasant and sanguine, and in the next, without any warning, an anti-Semitic slur slips off the tongue like a knocked-over glass of red wine on a white carpet. I invariably cringe at those times, flushing with indignation, then fearing the imagined flare-up ahead. I'm conditioned to such remarks and feel on edge when I hear them. Slurs test my spiritual levels of compassion, equanimity, and forgiveness. They make me scan where and how God lives within me. I flinch at the shock-jock word as if it were a punch heading my way. The word. In the beginning was the Word. Words hurt. Words heal. Words haunt. Words break people apart or bring them together. Words create a world that the speaker hopes to shape by inspir-ing or mesmerizing the listener.

~

Ages ago, the wildcat controlled his world to a greater degree. No more. He is at the mercy of whatever words and ideas human beings have about wildcat habitat. Facing each other, we hang suspended like time on a summer day, back east, July, 95 degrees, beaded sweat brow. Between us is a meadow. His genetic memory tells him to be wary of me, and why not? Why should he trust me, given what my species has done to his home? Synapses firing, ready, geared for fight or flight, the bob-cat knows that the forest is just a few leaps away, knows from experience that the two-legged one won't advance into a briar-wood. He's right: for the most part I cleave to the trail, an open space that signals safety and familiarity, an ordered haven from the tangled snares of the forest floor. I had learned that lesson once in New Hampshire, when I left the trail to shortcut a walk into town but soon became disoriented and lost. Hours of worry later, I stumbled upon a stream and followed it down through the thick forest to where it crossed a road—an urban trail.

This time, though, I take a step off the trail into the snags and pulls and tangles—greed, I guess, to get a better look, to see how close I can get. (Guys have a tendency to competition and will create opportunities even when no other human is around.) The cat bounds away even before my forward foot touches the ground. How often, during Buddhist walking meditation, I've watched the million movements my feet made. What good does that do me now, as I try to stalk silence in the real world?

Nothing in or around the trail is in conflict—at least, not conflict as humans know and create it. Even predator and prey have an agreement of sorts. The mole knows the dangers and threats to its survival as it pops out of its hole to lunch on a dandelion. Quail can sense the presence of the bobcat. The brush rabbit twists its eye to the sky on constant alert for the hawk. All have behaviors and disguises and colors and calls to help them survive. When the harrier hawk flashes its white-banded tail as it dives to impale and kill its bird, he may leave some feathers behind, but no hard feelings. The victim's compatriots do not issue a call to arms and advance on revenge raids against the hawks. No anger or regret or retribution. Life in the forest continues with no pause to label one event harmful and another harmonious.

Some might think, "How terrible—this violence, this primitive survival of the fittest." They compare a pile of feathers from an eaten warbler with a mugging or a drive-by shooting or a fight in a bar. They project human emotions onto the natural order of the woods. To be sure, prey may feel fear just before the predator's talons or teeth penetrate. The victim may resist or try to flee as the attack commences. But even if the prey escapes, it feels no revenge response, as with humans. Prey and predator return to their routine without any residue of animosity. In the woods, détentes consummated over millions of years have resulted in accommodation and moderation among all who live there. The earth quakes and cracks and heaves over time, and the nonhuman sentient beings who live on its surface adjust, adapt, change, evolve, and become adept at meeting challenges.

"Every adversity has within it the seed of an equal or greater benefit," said motivational writer Napoleon Hill in *Grow Rich with Peace of Mind*. The natural life around the trail knows that well, but, if it could speak, it would substitute "every natural event" for "adversity." Nature doesn't create reality but responds ably to its ever-changing conditions. Unlike people, who are constantly trying to make things happen, the trail receives whatever comes. It rejects nothing, nor does it judge, or choose, or lament what it gets. It represents "the meek" of the Beatitudes, and the trail is indeed a beneficiary of an inheritance that it is willing to share. The trail and its surrounding forest are rich beyond any human concept of wealth.

So I meet this meek trail with a meek heart, a heart willing to listen, to receive, to submit, even to surrender. This doesn't come easily to a Westerner like me. To be "meek," most of us think, means to be weak and groveling like a cowed dog. We would rather take charge, act, move on, progress, assert, ascend, upgrade, augment, succeed, go for it, or just "do it." The thought "I must have" has become a battle cry in the postwar world as consumers and entrepreneurs charge and conquer hill after hill in the name of progress—while losing sight, as soldiers often do, what they are fighting for. The result is the kind of excess that brings despair as we realize that the well of wanting can never be filled—and that, even if it were, happiness would not necessarily follow. Our insatiable human wanting has denuded forests, concretized farmland, and imprisoned us on rush-hour freeways. It has created a society that is too fast, too medicated, and too violent, with too little time to spend with families, friends, or selves. Is this what we truly want, or has the juggernaut completely lost its brakes?

~

On Sky Trail, I can leave that world and enter one that honors a slower pace, a world where I can browse through a shop of thoughts, words, feelings, and actions, taking time and choosing each mental item carefully, savoring the form and function of each. A warehouse of silence is there, in pinecones and skull-caps and the movement of slugs, in the glide of a red-tailed hawk, the dive of a black-shouldered kite, the brush-beat of a flying flock of crows.

I try to follow the bobcat into the forest, try to stifle the noise of nylon as I walk, to listen for the rustle of needles and leaves. How could it steal off without a sound? What magic is this to walk like an angel unfettered by earth? For one brief yet abundant moment, I hear the sound of sounds, the sound of silence. I stand there naked in that sound. For one precious moment, I am nothing and everything at once. Without seeking it, I am silence and the Grail is again in my hand, in my heart.

In the next moment, I become aware of that magnificent silence and the spell breaks. I am again a man, in and of time, with hopes, fears, desires, but something has changed. In that unbidden flash of recognition, I have realized that I am not alone and never will be alone. And isn't that our greatest fear? Isn't that the fear behind our fear of death? Isn't that the emotional engine that powers the pistons of desire and distraction? We feel a vacuum that we call boredom, we fill it with all manner of distractions, we look for palliatives to cure ourselves—but the treatment creates yet a larger vacuum as we become ever more lost to ourselves and to the true spirit behind our breath. The illusion of aloneness is the veil that comes between human beings and this swinging, dancing, singing, laughing, loving universe whose spherical bodies are "having a ball," as Alan Watts put it.

I have not sought this silence. Perhaps spiritual paths can pave the way, can clear the debris and make ready, but it is only when the path and its purpose are forgotten that true silence can bloom. And no path can teach us how to forget. Forgetting oneself is a blessing granted only through grace, that divine elegance that we see in dandelion seed balls and redwood cones and orb webs at dawn. Grace is the seed within the seed, that element that embodies both origin and present moment and laces them together with fine, fantastically delicate, yet strong thread. When I forget this self that separates me from grace, silent and alive as a seed that directs its taproot toward my soul, I remember the purpose of this life.

EXPLORING YOUR PATH

> The next time you walk in nature, slow your steps. Take in all that you see, smell, and hear. At times, let yourself stop walking as you close your eyes and just listen.

> Go outside with your journal and a magnifying glass, if you have one, and sit on the ground for a while. Begin to observe a small piece of Earth, perhaps a square yard or so, in front of you. Close your eyes. What do you hear? Open your eyes. What do you see? Breathe in. What do you smell? Take a few minutes to describe your sensory experiences in your journal. Look at the grasses, sticks, stones, and insects. Really see them. Touch the ground. Let yourself get close to Earth and smell the soil and the plants. Use your hand lens to observe even more closely. Take as much time as you need to record your experiences, thoughts, and feelings.

> Try stalking a wild animal or bird, perhaps a rabbit, a crow, a deer, a lizard, a trout, a great blue heron. How quiet can you be? How patient can you be? How empty of thought can you be? How still can you be? See how close you can get before the animal leaves. Teach a child these lessons in stillness.

Moon on the Man

Awareness of Earth is first felt through the feet, but seldom do we notice our essential contact with the Earth, our actual groundedness. We notice primarily the terrain—whether it is trail, sidewalk, lot, or street—and seldom feel its variety, its slope, grade, grain, and texture.

The winter rain carves small rivulet canyons on the trail. As steady and gentle as breath, the rain puts me into a mood different from the one I was in when I arrived. As always, it quiets me, allows me to hear my heartbeat. Earlier today, as I went about my Saturday errands all rubberized and insulated, and moving at speeds better suited to a machine, I was too frenzied to hear anything so delicate as my heartbeat. Perhaps that is actually how fast I should be moving—fast enough to do what needs to be done but still able to feel and hear my heart. Moving at such a pace, I could reply, "Yes, it's a good day," to someone who might inquire about my day. "I heard my heart."

I like slowing the pace of life. I like the perspective it affords of time lived. Objectively, all life lives at the same pace. It's the mind that makes differences. Time speeds by or lags depending on how much or what we are doing. Busyness clouds our awareness of our feelings, thoughts, and senses, and creates the illusion that time rules us. What results is a continuous chain of beginnings, a venerating of the new to the exclusion of the old that obliterates our awareness of each moment as an interweaving of endings and beginnings. But on and around the trail, both endings and beginnings cycle in harmony, in awareness, in renewal.

During the time of the full moon, I look forward to the ending of daylight like a child longing for a toy he knows his uncle will bring. I plan my walk for daylight throughout so I can see all the glories of the trail. Still, planning builds a wall around time and spontaneity. We spend so much time planning our time and even planning to plan our time, as when couples agree to set aside time to plan their weekend. And plans can sound good when drafted, but when the time comes to carry them out, we may be in a different mood, or perhaps we're not feeling well, but because of our ironclad plan, we feel compelled to follow through.

Through the years, I've missed much moonlight because I had other plans. But eventually, my craving turns into a beckoning serenade and I ache for the moonshadows of pine, fir, and madrone. I sweep away all my plans and go. I pack a dinner and start out, allowing enough time to see the sunset and moonrise from atop Mount Wittenberg. Who needs more "entertainment"? Who needs moving pictures of things? Who needs Web sites and Internets? They can never connect me with the world as much or as well as this evening walk can.

As the sun sinks, the animals stir. When I lived in New Hampshire, I rarely saw any wild animal larger than a squirrel or the occasional porcupine or beaver. In California and other Western states, though, I have seen deer, elk, otter (in a creek near the park), bobcat, fox, coyote, bear (including a grizzly in Montana), mountain goat, bighorn sheep (both mountain and desert), bison, marmot, mole, muskrat, ferret, feral pig, and once what I think was a cougar. That happened one winter evening on Sky Trail, in the murky and fading light of dusk, when I saw a large, dark shape pad off into the woods just off the trail as I returned from a hike. I knew that a deer would have bolted and that no bears roamed there at that time. I followed, hoping for a better look, but then I remembered stories about threatened cougars attacking people and backed off.

The cougar, classified under *Felis concolor* and known variously as puma, mountain lion, panther, painter, deer tiger, and catamount, is my spirit animal—my alter ego in the natural world who offers me true entry into that world. I long to see this special relative more than any other.

The cougar, still untamed and relatively untouched, touches a primordial core that civilized people gave up around the Industrial Revolution in exchange for safety and predictability. A few years ago, California's electorate banned sport hunting of the big cat and, consequently, hunters with dog packs are no longer permitted to track, tree, trap, and shoot them. The cougar has multiplied and prospered and reinhabited much of its original range, yet is still so elusive that sightings are rare. It can grow as big as a pickup truck, nose to tail, and is second only to the rare jaguar as the largest wildcat in North America. Its tawny coat blends perfectly with the palomino hills of the California summer, and it hunts mostly at night when no humans are near. Experienced trackers or wildlife photographers must lure the lion in with deer roadkill for bait. Many of the pictures of cougars in magazines are gotten that way, or are photos of cats kept captive in wildlife parks. In its natural habitat, the cougar is thoroughly wild, and each one will cover from 20 to as many as 100 miles in a day. It roams alone, or with a cub, and has a variety of calls that resemble a house cat's "but magnified many times in volume and depth of tone," according to the late biologist Olaus Murie in his *Field Guide to Animal Tracks*. The cougar trains its cubs in the ways of the wild for three years before sending them out on their own.

The possibility of seeing a cougar focuses me on those days when I approach the trail so cloistered in self-absorption and so tangled in my story of the moment that I cannot see Eden. But Eden—as teacher, as mentor, as lover—needs attention.

In the moonlight, when the sharp edges of day melt like ice in a sudden thaw, I see more clearly—in Don Juan's sense of seeing not with the eyes but with an inner knowing. The fading light forces me to reconfigure my orientation to the world. At dusk, when living things stir, the eyes become unreliable. A reclusive night heron floats through the sky like a ghost and whistles its high-pitched call on its way to estuarial haunts. Two owls atop the ridge hoot and chat. Crows fly low in formation, their wings sounding a soft kettledrum beat as they seek a resting place for the night. Deer, grazing in a nearby meadow a moment before, vanish the moment I turn my head to see the setting sun. Bats swoop and dive across the trail's air space, and old wives' tales interrupt my moment of peace.

In the east, low above the rolling hills dyed pink by the setting sun, the moon appears like a pearl on a jeweler's velvet cushion. I bring out my dinner. I eat like a beggar—fast, efficiently, mindlessly, biting and masticating, crunching and champing. The rising moon and setting sun should have been enough nourishment. The moment I finish, I forget what I've eaten.

A brief, feeble wind tries to gather a minyan but weakens into a dead calm. Slow, purple silence begins to fill the sky. That time between the two worlds of day and night triggers the atavistic knowledge that dark is at hand and, like a child at bedtime, I look for something familiar to hold on to. The dark will erase the reassuring sights and landmarks that distract me from feeling the aloneness that can easily fray into loneliness.

As the sun touches the headlands to the west, the pace of its setting is easily measured against the land horizon. I feel wistful, the way I used to when we sang "Taps" at the end of evening campfire programs in summer camp when I was a boy.

All the setting suns I've seen drain like sand in the hourglass of a life. Eating distracts me from the twinge of fear that this thought arouses. One final flash of light flares as the sun seems to change its mind, seems about to return, and then it's gone, in unison with my last bite of whatever it was. The curtain descends but leaves enough light that I can continue to look outward instead of inward, at my soul. I sit in receptive silence. A small gust heralds the night.

~

Looking back, I don't remember fearing the night when I was a child. I always liked my room as dark as possible. For me, there were never any monsters in the closet or under the bed. When we still lived in my grandparents' house in South Philadelphia, I had my own room and was never afraid of the night.

Once we moved to Wynnefield, I shared a room with Hank and bedtime was even cozier and more fun because of his willingness, even though he was so much older than I, to talk with me about the happenings of the day, particularly sports. After dinner and homework, we would watch our favorite shows, have some milk and cake, and then get into our beds and turn off the lights, with one of us whispering, "Let's talk." It was comforting, loving, and sweet, and I looked forward to the dark and to our conversations, however mundane.

Then the wheel turned and things changed. A few years later, my brother went off to college and eventually got married. This became a blessing for me because, as our family splintered, his wife Judy became at times the only person I could confide in. Bubbe and Zeyde were dead. My mother and father disappeared emotionally. Alone now, I would drift off to sleep, only to awaken in the middle of a recurring nightmare in which my body, expanding like a balloon, seemed about to float away into space. Now, as night approached, I was terrified that I would have the dream again, and I would cry myself to sleep—lonely, scared, abandoned. For years, the feeling of my body expanding would sometimes continue into the day, perhaps the result of my trying to suppress difficult feelings. The night was no longer comforting, but, when the dream finally stopped, darkness remained a refuge where I could feel my sadness, slip off to sleep, and have a few hours' respite.

All this came back to haunt me a few years later when I began suffering from my debilitating anxiety disorder and agoraphobia. By then Donna and I were married—a harmonious union of two old friends. I longed for night, which brought me relief from my emotional suffering. Sleep was pure escape, and the darker and quieter the room, the better. But our marriage could not withstand my angst and, after six years, it dissolved in 1975. I moved to a roach-infested though affordable apartment in Boston to finish my master's degree in counseling, and moved again, and again, each time to a place darker and safer at night than the one before, until finally I found the darkest place possible.

Two years after Donna and I separated, I moved to the cabin in New Hampshire. It had no electricity, plumbing, telephone, streetlights, or even a street. The two miles that separated me from the main road put me far enough in the woods that I had as much nighttime silence and darkness as I wanted, aside from the occasional airplane flyover, snowmobile, or chainsaw. During my four years there, my relationship with the night regained the peace I had felt as a little boy surrounded by my loving family and talking about nothing much with Hank late at night in our beds.

~

Two or three hours before sunset, the air seems heavy, as if having absorbed all the day's collective running-around energy, the worries, the doubts, the petty peeves, the affronts, the putdowns of self and others that, taken all together, disrespect both love and life. The dusk gathers and stills and settles my consciousness like precipitate sinking to the bottom of a test tube. In the ocean-fresh air of the trail, my breathing comes more easily and I notice it more, perhaps because the woods themselves heave and contract like one large chest. This noticing is an epiphany of sorts, as is awareness of all simple, profound events. In the charged air, I become conscious of the embroidery of breath—its feathery textures, its hues that match the soft, changing greens of the fir forest, its pace that makes me feel more human, more comfortable with my Is-ness, my Such-ness, my I-Thou-ness, my That-ness. Perhaps Alan Watts was right in suggesting that when babies say "Da-da-da," they're not saying "Da-da" or "Daddy," as fathers would like to think, but rather "That, That, That," in awe and acknowledgment of all in view.

Darkness follows the setting sun, quietly, imperceptibly, and then, at a certain point, almost suddenly. One moment, I can see my feet and the next I can't. I'm always caught a bit off-guard by that point of darkness that defines the night, that forces my senses to shift from the visual to the aural and tactile. The familiar landmarks I habitually use to define myself in relation to my environment are gone, and, without my eyes to guide me, I must attune myself to an inner, higher frequency.

There appear to be two eyes staring at me from the brush. The eyes of Spirit, a Miwok might say, manifested through Bobcat or Cougar or Coyote. In the night, the mystical, the sacred, is more available. The forest comes alive. Owls converse more freely. Feeling safer, small critters emerge from underground homes to find food. Larger animals lie in wait, seizing upon the smallest lapse in attention of their prey.

It's rare to find other people in the forest after dark. Most hurry to return to their cars and roads while some daylight remains. They flee as if some evil were dogging their footsteps, perhaps remembering and heeding the cautionary notes about cougars posted at the trailhead. I've been more wary myself since seeing that large, dark, sleek shadow slipping off into the woods. In fact, I've had several fantasies of *Felis concolor* jumping me from behind. In one, a terrific battle ensues as "The Ballad of Davy Crockett" plays in my head and provides inspiration (especially the lines about how Davy, my childhood hero, killed a bear when he was three).

The cougar bites my neck, but I've somehow gotten out my trusty knife. I slit his underbelly from sternum to scrotum and he drops dead on top of me. I am relieved, exhausted, but somehow exhilarated. That's one scenario of the hero's journey. The other, more cerebral and metaphysical, draws inspiration from the Buddha who, during one of his past lives, threw himself to a starving tiger so the animal could eat and survive. So much for the thoughts spawned during nice, peaceful evening walks in the woods.

Cougars, bats, owls, eyes—the night promises no safety or security. It pushes on my old fears like blood in a blister. It tests faith stripped of reassuring light, but anything that tests faith potentially strengthens me if I rise to meet the test head-on. How will I react to the fear of the unknown, to the dangers ratcheted to the surface of consciousness by my catastrophizing mind? Fear and anxiety have stalked me from birth; they're part of my family legacy. I've run before, and running is still the first impulse, a knee-jerk reaction as the message of danger crackles through my synapses like a thousand firecrackers exploding at once. I heard someone joke recently that Chi Gong and Tai Chi were not the world's oldest martial arts—running was.

And I would have run, but for the moon chinning itself up and over the eastern horizon. It is huge at first, an optical illusion caused by the refraction of light near the horizon. Around me, light returns, more subdued than daylight but defining the landscape once again. Darkness shrouds the boundaries between things, and without such distinctions the conscious, conditioned mind gets disoriented and fearful. On trails I'm comfortable with, like the Sky, I like to expand my limits at times and saunter quietly on moonless nights. Spiritual work is often about soaring to new heights, repeating affirmations, doing good works, striving for enlightenment. Soul work is about digging to deeper levels, stirring up and poking into the ashes in the kitchen, as I heard Robert Bly and Michael Meade say once at a men's retreat. On this trail, at night, both are possible. Still, the night does have its dangers. On one moonless jaunt with a woman friend, I failed to take my flashlight. But night walking requires impeccable concentration, and, caught up in walking and talking, I lost my footing and fell hard onto a ledge 10 feet below the trail. We were at a spot on the Coast Trail, near the Palomarin trailhead at the south end of the park, where the drop-off was 200 feet to the ocean in some places. Drawn away from my body by conversation, I was also cut off from the inherent Earth-wisdom of the body—a dangerous situation that actually did result in my friend breaking her arm and me spraining my ankle. So night walking is best done only when we can pay full attention to signals from our body and senses.

Moonlight reassures and tempers the uncertain night. Familiar trees and trail signs become visible again. I hike higher on the Sky, a steady climb, but with plateaus along the way that gives my heart respite from hoisting my 180 pounds of human flesh and bone. I notice landmarks everywhere. A rocky spine where the trail branches higher starts me fantasizing about prehistoric skeletons embedded in the granite. A horseshoe bend at the end of a canyon where cold air in winter alchemizes into a warm draft and, in the warm fall, the warm air mixing and swirling in the bowl of the bend feels colder. The muddy patches from summer fog dripping off fir needles. A wet spot where dripping spring water finds its lowest level. The coarse, weathered groundcover on Wittenberg's summit. The trail to the summit was once a hard pull up a steep, sandy slash, but after the 1995 fire it was engineered into a gentler switchback that guides me to the top in a few quickened heartbeats.

What is it about the sight of the full moon that thrills, that draws even the city dweller's attention from the street? I've seen people glance up in the heaviest of Boston traffic to admire the moon before returning to the fray to cut someone off. Perhaps anything that lights up the night attracts us. And because anything that lightens the ominous darkness makes the night more familiar and makes us feel safer.

Perhaps our attraction to the moon also arises from its mystery, its place in myth and story and song, even if these go no further back than our own childhood. Egyptians learned about Thoth, the god of the moon, and his wife Maat, who weighed the hearts of the dead against a feather, and allowed those whose hearts were light as that feather to enter heaven. Americans and Western Europeans may remember stories of the man in a moon made of green cheese and rhymes like "Hey-diddle-diddle, the cat and the fiddle, the cow jumped over the moon." So, like children, we glance up and for a moment relive the days when the moon and its myths grabbed our full attention.

Perhaps it is also the moon's link with love that lures our eyes and thoughts. Romance remembered softens the crustiness of routine. Gazing at the enchanted moon, I remember a moment of quiet sharing with a woman I once loved. We eventually parted, but the moon jogs my memory and "re-hearts" me as the sight "re-minds" me. Of course, love can also lead to lunacy—the term comes from Luna, the Roman moon-goddess.

~

Rising gradually, the moon begins to dominate the sky above Wittenberg. The rosy hues that linger around it from the setting sun are soft and inviting, so easy on the eyes. My seeing could linger there forever. At illumined times like these I like to dance the ancient Tai Chi, that play of movements that the Chinese Taoists developed by observing aspects of nature. I used to have a purpose when I did Tai Chi—I hoped that it would bring me peace and oneness—but now I offer it more as a prayer and in gratitude for all the nature, in its oneness and glory, that lies before, behind, and all around me.

That oneness always is and always will be, a birthright for all beings. It is that which has never been born and will never die. It cannot be sought, bought, bargained for, or traded. You cannot train for it, practice it, imitate it, or pretend you have it. Once realized, it will not bring you wealth, fame, health, or happiness. What it will do is awaken you to your eternal bond with everything in the universe. And once you know this, your insides will turn inside out and in every interaction, you will face yourself—and in facing yourself, you will face squarely all of life around you. This is the first step in loving yourself and loving all of nature.

On the morning of the Buddha's enlightenment, he opened his eyes and saw the planet Venus, the morning star, low in the sky with his soul's eye. At that moment, he realized nirvana, the state of complete liberation that obliterates the necessity for continuing on the ever-turning wheel of birth and death. But he chose instead to stay and teach others the path to that freedom and compassion. He fell in love with the world and all life, as did Jesus and Mohammed and Kabir and Rumi and Mirabai and Kahlil Gibran and Francis of Assisi and Thomas Merton and Martin Luther King Jr. and Mother Teresa and Peace Pilgrim and the Dalai Lama and Moses and Abraham and Ruth and

Isaac and Black Elk and Crazy Horse and Krishnamurti and Einstein and John Muir and Julia Butterfly and Albert Schweitzer and Martin Buber and Florence Nightingale and Clara Barton and Lincoln and Sacagawea and Jimmy Carter and Hildegard of Bingen and William Wordsworth and William Blake and Rainer Marie Rilke and Han-Shan and Basho and Count Basie and Ella Fitzgerald and Ray Charles and Eleanor Roosevelt and Thoreau and Gandhi and Sojourner Truth and Viktor Frankl and Ralph Waldo Emerson and the young diarist Opal Whiteley and Stevie Wonder and George Washington Carver and Lao Tsu and Meister Eckhart and Walt Whitman and Ramana Maharshi and Luther Burbank and Suzuki Roshi and Pope John XXIII and King David and Nelson Mandela.

When we fall in love with the world, it is natural to want to stick around and help out, not to improve our karma or place in the cosmic order but to make things better, to help others on the arduous journey. Buddha wasn't a meditator—he was an authentic person in communion with the world, as are all those listed above as well as many others not mentioned.

~

As I dance the Tai Chi on Wittenberg summit at dusk, with the full moon rising and the sun setting in a cushion of pastel softness, I am in prayer and gratitude for the synchronicity that brings me to this spot at this time. And the blessings I feel meld into these movements learned from ancient ones. First I bow, my palms together, to the magnificence before me. Suzuki Roshi, the late abbot of the San Francisco Zen Center, devoted a chapter to bowing in his classic *Zen Mind, Beginner's Mind*. "By bowing we are giving up ourselves," he wrote, "...But when you bow to Buddha you should have no idea of Buddha, you just become one with Buddha, you are already Buddha himself. When you become one with Buddha, one with everything that exists, you find the true meaning of being."

Then, quietly, my arms rise like wings and settle with my palms flat toward the ground, triggering a series of movements that flow one from the other as gracefully as a heron's flight— Wild Horse Ruffling Mane, White Crane Flapping Wings, Stepping Back and Repulsing the Monkey, Grasping the Sparrow's Tail. My favorite is Cloud Hands, where my legs sweep left while my hands move in opposite circles up and above my brow as my eyes scan the horizon. I feel like a hawk, and I invariably see red-tails and turkey vultures from this aerie soaring along the coastal currents down into the valleys and over the ridge. Cloud Hands usually goes for three cycles but I often extend it to cover the whole flat area at the summit that looks out past the headlands to the Pacific Ocean, spread out before me like a million diamonds on a cloth of velvet.

The Tai Chi lightens me, unburdens me of this dense body that encases this busy mind. In Cloud Hands, my outer vision softens while my inner eye sees with laser precision. This favorite movement, like all other Tai Chi movements, is in total union with life. Cloud Hands does not resist, nor does it try to change anything, nor does it purport to accept or reject anything, nor does it try to understand or explain or answer any questions I may have brought to the trail. This movement is a prayer—an expression of grace that has no other purpose than gratitude for the supreme blessing of being able to experience, with heart and soul, life as it is. Any veneer of purpose clouds the beauty of life itself. Simple. Awake. Alive. Cloud Hands welcomes all—the day, the setting sun, the night, the moon, and the rising sun, with an open heart.

"Every day is a good day," said Dogen, the 13th-century master who founded the Soto School of Zen. Think it through—if we have only a limited number of days, aren't they all good? The Inuit said the same thing in a different way with this ancient, simple, and elegant song.

EARTH PRAYERS FROM AROUND THE WORLD

And I thought over again
My small adventures
As with a shore-wind I drifted out
In my kayak
And thought I was in danger,

My fears,
Those small ones
That I thought so big
For all the vital things
I had to get and to reach.

And yet, there is only
One great thing,
The only thing:
To live to see in huts and on journeys
The great day that dawns,
And the light that fills the world.

EXPLORING YOUR PATH

> Take a walk in the moonlight in some natural place where you can see a lot of sky, and let the light of the moon illuminate your way. What comes to mind and heart? Fear? Courage? Comfort? Love? Childhood memories? Take a little time afterwards to record your impressions, thoughts, feelings, and insights in your journal.

> What is your relationship to the night? Think back to your childhood and recall any experiences that shaped this relationship. Has it changed? If you had a positive connection, do you still honor it by spending time outside in the night? If your connection was negative, spend some time thinking about the reasons, and consider ways in which you could begin to approach the night from a new perspective.

> Consider learning some basic Tai Chi or Chi Gong from an instructor, a book, or a video. Experience what it feels like when you practice in a comfortable place in nature.

Grace Land

Today I walk slowly at a pace that permits memories, feelings, and tears to overtake the busyness of my walking. It is early March; a stiff wind and shady spots chase my hands into my pockets. Usually Sky Trail is a good wind trail—a place where fir and pine, dense and tall, subdue the blowing air and offer an oasis of sun and warmth on chilly winter and early spring days. Huckleberry blossoms color the undergrowth with pink flowers that dangle like tiny lanterns. Their numbers and vibrant color herald a good crop come fall.

The winter brought regular rains at intervals that minimized flooding in the lowland towns, but mud still puddles on parts of the trail and forces me off-trail a bit to balance along the slippery edges of deep gullies made green by the rains. Douglas iris, the first I've seen this year, blooms blue as the shell of a robin's egg. This vernal harbinger sprouts near the huckleberries and under some huge firs in a sunny patch of long and wild grasses just off the trail. To the Greeks, Iris was the personification of rainbows and a messenger of the gods. As the gatekeeper of truth, she carried water in an urn from the River Styx when the gods had to take an oath. If they broke their oath, Iris would pour the water upon them and render them unconscious for a year. On this trail too, she is truth—the first flower, related to the crocus, and with the start of the spring dance, all is conscious and alive as the dancers take their first steps.

I walk aware of each step, of the grade of the hill pulling on my thighs, of the movement of the bones and cartilage in my knees making my aging joints ache at times. To walk in this deliberate manner is not physically difficult, for my heart is comfortable with such a pace and the knee pain is tolerable, but the slowness coaxes tender emotions to surface and brings me eye to eye with "I." My mind bids my body, "Go faster!" It is impatient with the tightened rein I impose. With automobiles and airplanes and TV and telephones and digital electronics and computer technology, I, like most of us today, have been trained for speed. This training often has me racing up the trail, pausing at the top, and then racing back down, hurrying to get somewhere or see someone or do something that I think will be gone or that I'll miss or lose out on if I don't get there fast enough.

On this day, I have not consciously decided to resist that conditioning; I go slowly because my heart is too heavy to allow my body to move fast. On this day, Thomas Moore's saturnine place in the garden, "...a dark, shaded, remote place where a person could retire and enter the persona of depression without fear of being disturbed...," is not a corner of the trail but the way I walk. My gait is deliberate, measured, slow, labored, heavy. With each step, I feel the effort of my legs hoisting the weight of my body. The lugubrious "Song of the Volga Boatmen" is Number One on my Saturn Top 40. My steps disdain distance traveled, time past, or time to come. They are an expression of grief.

A word from my mother triggered the feeling, a snippet of armchair analysis in which she purported in one line to explain a complex series of actions and reactions by equally complex players over a period of years in my life. It was something about how I had allowed the women I had married to control all my significant life decisions. Of course, her words contained more than one nugget of truth, but what she overlooked was that when my marriages had finally become intractable, I had been the one to reassume control of my life and had made the decision to divorce.

It wasn't so much her words but the dynamics of our communication that had darkened my mood. She thrust—I parried. She poked—I ducked. We were demonstrating, all too expertly, the all-too-common attacker-defender pattern. Our responses were as ritualized as an English tea. They also stirred memories of similar communication struggles my first wife and I had shared. We married in 1969 after having been close friends for four years in college. Seven years later—a year after we divorced, she took a chalice of pills, deadly as hemlock, and killed herself. She had moved out of our old apartment that day, and her new housemate came home that evening to find her lying lifeless on her bed. Thinking about her always brought tears to my eyes as I remembered the love we had once shared. This time, though, as I walked slowly, the small tears intensified as I thought of her death and our lost marriage.

Grief defies all panaceas and prescriptions. With grief, there are no sure fixes—no specific exercises in creative visualization, or sessions with a grief counselor, or even accepting Elisabeth Kubler-Ross's stages, however useful all these may be. After Donna died, I spent a lot of time in therapy—Bioenergetics and Gestalt and Rebirthing and Psychodrama. But with some deaths—sudden deaths like accidents, heart attacks, murders, an operation gone wrong, soldiers in wartime, or the suicide of someone you loved and lived with—resolution can take a long, long time, if it ever comes at all.

We used to walk together, she and I, around a pond out in the country where we lived in Wrentham, a small, classic New England town just southwest of Boston. One day I took her picture. Barefoot, she tucked her thumbs into the pockets of her tomboy jeans, her white T-shirt tucked in tight and sexy. Her smile said, "I like this world. I like you. I like me. I'm happy we're together." I kept the picture for years but finally burned it, along with all our courtship love letters, in a big bonfire when I left my New Hampshire cabin four years after she died.

We used to walk together, she and I, talking about a future that never came.

~

Hunched over like a crone, I snake up the trail, past the lone iris, the budding huckleberries, the " tulgey" Lewis Carroll woods, all tangled in Spanish moss and poison oak and "Jabberwock" briar, the "brillig" meadow where the "Bandersnatch" bobcat stalks, the dead Bishop pine, the knoll at the top of one rise festooned with forget-me-nots as blue and perky as a bevy of bridesmaids, past wide views of Mount Vision where the fire started. I see little of all this because my eyes are awash in tears that drip on my cheeks like a watercolor sky applied too early. What was that relationship all about? How does love crumble into resentment and hostility? Or is it something else that changes? Or does nothing change at all? What happened to the love that I felt for her when our marriage was strong and supple? Did that love change after our divorce, after her death, after my subsequent relationships?

The grief I've carried to the trail is not for the loss of anything or anyone. Perhaps it isn't grief at all, but rather a deep connection with love, an accumulated love from all the love I have ever felt—not a romantic love but a love that filled my entire being, a love that sometimes got lost in the din of days. Perhaps I am not grieving the loss of love but realizing that love was always present and that those I've loved, alive or dead, were present in that current of eternal love. I could remember someone from 30 years before and deep inside, in that place where love lives, I could feel love not only for that person but for all life.

As I continue my slow steps, my awareness of this great love germinates like a seed sown and nurtured. Could this be why children dawdle and cats nap, or why lovers dreamily walk to nowhere, or why people like to gaze at the ocean?

~

One spur of Sky Trail, the Horse Trail, forks left and leads up to the summit. The charred bark of old-growth fir reminds me that the fire of 1995 singed this area. It was once a sliver of a path, fringed with prickly thistle and rattlesnake grass, winding up through a dense canopy, with good mud in spots. The firefighters bulldozed it into a wide firebreak, but three years of nature's care has nursed it back to almost its original condition. I begin to notice the quiet where trees block the wind near a fork with the Z Ranch Trail, which ascends up the ridge. A sunny patch warms me. The warmth is comforting, and for a moment my tears stop, paving the way for the action of grace that lies at the core of the trail and its natural life.

Grace itself has no core. It has no beginning or end and so is a glimpse of eternity—that which has no boundaries, no limits. And that which has no limits always, simply, is. "If it ever struck you that you are a flash of awareness in the midst of eternal nothingness," wrote Alan Watts in *God*, "the flash would be the same as eternity because it would be all there is. There couldn't be anything outside of it. It couldn't even have ends or a beginning. Because there has to be something on the other side of a beginning and something on the other side of an end. You can't have a boundary at all if there's nothing on the outside of it."

In that patch of warmth, nothing exists, and, in that "nothing at all," all is perfect. Perhaps it isn't only the warmth, for grace does not just spring from the trail and its climate. It arises from the mix of trail, weather, tears, gait, and the longing of a stink beetle plodding across the path to mate with its partner. An infinite number of permutations and combinations in nature shape the action of grace in any given moment—my own emotional and cultural history, my dead ex-wife's, Bubbe's, my mother's, and the couple illegally walking their dog on the trail.

Grace defies conceptualization. I cannot control its arrival, or create, seek, or change it. Grace responds only to the genuine, the innocent, the unpretentious, the receptive—to the gentle heart that does not covet. All I can do, then, is attend fully to my present experience of being a human being, whether that consists of walking, crying, seeing, praying, or tying my shoelaces. Those moments, so conceived, are pure, open, limitless, and eternal, worthy of the arrival of grace. And in them, I transcend the boundaries of this material plane and touch that True Place, that "just this moment," where all, alive or dead, ultimately reside.

~

The bright, sunny spot soon gives way to a brisk wind on the ridge as I ascend. I start wishing I were warmer, and the spell breaks. To wish for anything other than what is, is to close up the space that allows grace to enter. And yet I can't practice being present with the intention of having more grace in my life. Grace has nothing to do with practice, and even to prepare for it assumes, wrongly, that you aren't already fully ready and deserving. Practice and preparation create boundaries and draw distinctions. Grace smashes them.

The only way out of gracelessness is to live authentically, yet even then there's no guarantee that grace will appear. When it comes to grace, you can't "Go for it" or "Make it happen" or "Just do it." Grace requires faith—not faith in something or someone, as we have been taught, but faith without object, faith that is as ordinary and, at the same time, extraordinary, as our every breath. Few have it because, instead of learning to trust our spiritual instincts and affinities, we have learned to doubt, which limits our capacity to love and be loved. Doubt corrodes faith, and without faith we are like the thief who steals to satisfy his own needs at the expense of another. As long as we doubt—ourselves, our community, our spirit of oneness with all that lives—our way home remains obscure.

As I look out to the Pacific from atop Wittenberg, I see how the mind becomes tangled in doubt. The process is subtle and was perhaps best described by Krishnamurti, whose way of meditating examined how passing thoughts cascade into solid and separate "things" that separate us from the world. He suggested looking at the origins of self by seeing how thought begins, how "I" arises after perception, concept, discrimination, and categorization. By catching that "I" early, he suggested, we can nip that separation from the world in the bud.

So I gaze at the land and seascape spread out before me like a vast mural, and I begin to think about how the ocean has always been a confidant for me, particularly before my first marriage, when I went to Cape Cod and…and my mind is off and running. I lasso the thought and return to "I see the ocean…" My eyes see the light and color reflected off the ocean before my mind labels that phenomenon as "ocean" and, in that moment of seeing, I and the light and the color and the ocean are connected, without any words to separate us. Doubt does not exist, and gradually, over time, in my being with and in nature, my own doubt begins to dissipate and faith predominates. Nature is faith made manifest.

Of course, words and concepts and limits and fences define life in the conventional world, but if we see that world as primary, we become lost in those words and lost to our intimate connections and sacred roots. To see what is before thought is to shatter the illusion of separateness that leads to doubt, which annihilates faith, which blocks the door through which grace can enter. Sexual orgasm with someone we love is about as close as most of us come to all of this.

As the afternoon draws on, the wind begins gusting from the north, so I consider moving to a more sheltered spot. Changing body positions is simply a matter of desire—to be more comfortable, to be doing something more interesting, to escape the fear of thinking too much about things that my ego, concerned with survival, would rather not dwell upon. Trees and plants hold their basic positions. Their roots define their place, and they contend and are apparently content with whatever comes along. Unlike them, I am not rooted, and, because I have the option of moving, I am continually looking for a level of comfort that will bring me more contentment for a while, until I become uncomfortable again. If my mind right now didn't care about comfort or discomfort, I might sit here in stillness for hours, as I did during that 17-hour meditation years ago. But now I'm over 50 and my body wants warmth rather than cold, so I pull myself to my feet and descend.

EXPLORING YOUR PATH

> Go to your favorite trail and begin walking slowly, so slowly that people might almost think you're strange. Let your mind follow your body's lead as it settles and begins to clear. What feelings arise? What memories? This is a time to let down some of the defenses blocking you from seeing you and your True Self. When you return, take some time to record your impressions and insights in your journal.

> In what ways have you acted authentically recently? Can you think of any time when your thoughts, feelings, and actions were organic, whole, all of a piece? What did that feel like? If you can't remember any such occurrence, can you think of a recent situation you could have handled differently, so that you could have been more authentic? How can you place attention on acting more authentically in the future?

> From your perspective, what is grace? Have you ever felt it? Do you know how to open to it? Do you know how you might be blocking the door to its entering your life? Use your journal for this important exercise so that you can return to it from time to time and review your relationship to grace and living an authentic life.

Resurrection

Driving the winding Limantour Road, which bisects the heart of the park, had never before confronted me with peril until that dark night when I hit the doe. I had just finished hiking Sky Trail—later than I'd intended—and was racing home to do something—of great importance at the time, I'm sure, but ultimately of such little importance that I can no longer remember what it was. I was driving the unlit road near the trailhead faster than I should have, my brights on, crossing the double lines to cut the angles of the curves, when the deer leapt in front of my car.

The deer, all eyes and ears and legs, landed on top of the car as I slammed on the brakes and veered to a stop 50 yards down the road. When she hit, I felt the full force of her muscles, tendons, sinews, and bones, body parts I had never associated with a delicate, prancing doe. Then she flew off the hood and onto the shoulder of the road as if she'd been hit by a mortar shell. Stunned, I sat in my car and looked back, hoping that somehow the deer, like a cat miraculously scurrying off after being run over, would get to her feet and bound into the woods. I backed up my two-door Toyota and aimed its headlights toward the downed animal. She had not run off. She was lying there straining to raise her head. For a moment it looked as if she would rise on long, wobbly legs like a newborn colt and run off. I sat behind the wheel for many long moments praying for this to happen. She didn't move. Finally I got out of the car and walked toward her. Terrified, she tried to leap up but couldn't. She settled back down and laid her head on the ground. Perhaps at some deep level beyond knowing, she knew she was broken and would not rise again. The immense muscles of her hind legs quivered, then relaxed.

In that moment of impact, my life and hers joined. And when our eyes met, we became intimate, for in the meeting of eyes are the seeds of relationship. Our eyes drew us together so that we became one being connected on that plane where grace resides. In a magazine essay called "Apologia," naturalist Barry Lopez wrote that he always stops when he sees dead animals and moves "each one away from the tarmac into a cover of grass or brush out of decency, I think....Who are these animals, their lights gone out? What journeys have fallen apart here?"

I wished I could have revived her with a word, as they say Jesus did Lazarus, but there was nothing I could do. As soon as I got home, I called the Humane Society to report the accident. The doe had still been alive when I left, which fueled wishful thoughts that the rescuers could perform a miracle and save her. However, most of what humane societies do is scoop up the remains of dead animals, "put down" the injured and lost ("putting them out of their misery," as the saying has it), and dispose of the carcasses to shelter the public from its own guilt and complicity in the plight of these creatures. "We treat the attrition of lives on the road like the attrition of lives in war: horrifying, unavoidable, justified," Barry Lopez wrote. "Accepting the slaughter leaves people momentarily fractious, embarrassed."

~

Having to face that mangled body also made me question my blind acceptance of and participation in the cult of the motor vehicle, which reduces distances and time constraints but at such a high cost to the natural world. The road is the bastard child of the illicit affair between car and driver. The deer's instinct is to migrate—to breed or to feed or to return home for the night, and, after thousands of years, a road will not change that, no matter how dangerous the crossing. Animals on the move haven't got much of a chance.

But they persist. They must. They can't do anything else, but often a car, a truck, a motorcycle is there, too, and upon them before they can run, crawl, slither, leap, or hop out of harm's way. To be sure, walkers, joggers, birders, and bicyclists, too, are sometimes caught in the massacre as they vie with cars on country roads—but they at least know the score and can sometimes foresee the danger and save themselves.

To my knowledge, that was the first time that anything living (beside insects on my windshield) had ever gotten "in the way of" my car. The accident sickened me. It revived an old desire to "walkabout" on foot and do without an automobile. Was driving worth the carnage and the shock to our environment?

In New Hampshire, going on foot for two years enhanced my life. Although it was less convenient to get around, I developed a love of walking that has deepened over the years. In fact, I lived quite well back then because I had to be more efficient with my shopping. I relied on friends for rides when needed, and I hitchhiked, used the bus, bought a bicycle, worked close to home, cross-country skied, walked, saw more of my community and met people and cats I would have sped past before. The daily pace slowed. I savored more moments of life. Without a car, I needed less money, so I was able to cut back on salaried work and had more time for writing, music-making, reading, hiking, spending time with friends, even volunteering at a nearby nursing home. My stress levels went down, time for spiritual pursuits went up.

Is it possible to live a fulfilling life without a car? Love gave us life, and life gave us legs. That's all. Humans invented the car in a search for expediency and profit, and, in the process, conditioned a society to speed, convenience, and the way one looked behind the wheel. The ad boys had an easy time selling the public on the virtues of owning a car, especially with the advent of the affordable Ford. After World War II, the politico-corporate world engineered a society and an economy that depended on healthy car sales. Now people can buy cheaper houses in the suburbs—which requires commuting two or more hours to work, which in turn requires more, wider, straighter, and faster roads. Each year, the "highwaymen" annex more territory to create more automotive infrastructure....I'm ranting, I know. The car is probably here to stay (although we once said that of child labor in America and the Dodgers in Brooklyn and the Berlin Wall).

~

When I was a boy spending many summers at camp in the Poconos, I dreamed of seeing a deer in the woods. I'm not sure why I always considered the deer in such a reverential way, but this nature boy knew that he hadn't really been in the wild until he'd seen a wild, bounding deer. But I didn't see my first wild deer until I was 33, and then they were the "cookie crunchers" of Virginia's Shenandoah National Park that had become plentiful nuisances at rest stops and scenic overlooks because tourists insisted on giving them handouts. It was not until I moved to the West and discovered Sky Trail that I saw true wild deer, loping freely through meadow and wood, dependent on no human for sustenance. They epitomized grace, beauty, and harmony in motion. Around Sky Trail, the blacktail and the nonnative fallow and axis deer had it all—a beautiful and protected environment, few predators, a plentiful food supply, and only an occasional culling of the latter two species by park rangers to protect the native blacktails. The rangers usually did this unobtrusively, even using bow and arrow when possible, and then donated the meat to food banks in the city.

~

As a species, deer are not faring well worldwide. In East Asia, poachers hunt down the males in large numbers, leaving the carcasses to rot after they rip out the small musk bag from under the skin of the abdomen so they can sell it to perfumers eager to fulfill the world's desire for expensive fragrances. In Europe, the deer are nearing extinction because they are losing their habitat. In Africa, civilization continues to encroach on the wild lands that support deer and other mammals. In the United States, as hunting has declined and the deer's natural predators—

wolves, cougars, coyotes—have been decimated, the deer population in some suburban areas has proliferated to the edge of starvation due to too little food and the loss of wild habitat. This scenario is especially obvious on the Point Reyes peninsula, as is true for many areas in the United States, where most of the deer grow no bigger than large dogs due to hunting restrictions and the historical decline in numbers of the mountain lion. So the deer population has exploded, which creates intense competition for available food.

~

The doe relaxes some. Perhaps she is resigning herself to her fate. As long as I keep a certain distance, she lies still, as if bedded down for the night. I'm sure she senses that something is wrong, but she may not be aware of anything we call death. She must be feeling pain, but I doubt that she sees it as a harbinger of death, as I might. Instead, she seems to be waiting, instinctually trusting that nature will care for her.

At that moment, she seems more evolved than I, as I stand there worrying and wondering what to do, making a problem out of something essentially simple: A deer leapt in front of my car and, though I tried to brake, I could not avoid hitting it. She was dying, and I could not save her. I could only say "Om Mani Padma Hum," the Tibetan mantra of compassion that translates "Hail to the Jewel in the Lotus," drive on, and call the proper authorities when I got home. If only I could have stopped at sadness and regret, but my conditioned mind added remorse and guilt.

~

Two days later, I returned to the site. The deer was gone. I looked for signs of the carnage but none remained. All seemed in order. But my perception of the landscape had changed. Now, forevermore, my "innerscape" would see that deer and her terror at the moment of impact. Innocence lost, death faced, grace gained.

I have not given up my car, but I do drive the road more carefully and patiently now that I've been made so aware that death and grace are near and that this road benefits only one species, human beings, at the expense of many others. The road reminds me that nature pays a huge price for our conveyances and their infrastructures. I can acknowledge my responsibility in this self-absorbed scheme and pay homage to grace, which always hovers nearby waiting to teach its lessons of life. For grace can appear as suddenly as a squall or a deer four feet beyond a dashboard.

EXPLORING YOUR PATH

> The next time you see a dead animal lying on the side of the road, consider sending it a prayer and an apology. You may even want to stop your car when you do this so you can focus your full attention on this ritual. Bring attention to that being and its life and its family and how it died. Take a few minutes to write about your thoughts and feelings in your journal.

> Do some research on wildlife rescue and rehabilitation in your area. It would be good to have phone numbers, addresses, and people to contact in case you find an injured or abandoned animal that needs care. After all, most of their problems are human-created, so we must take responsibility for their welfare. Our lives are important, but so are theirs. Keep a record of all the animals you help, and, if you have children or grandchildren, consider sharing these wildlife interests with them.

> Do some research on other organizations, either regional or national, dedicated to conserving wild lands and life. Support them with your time and money.

Pain as Teacher

Imposing limits on personal behavior is anathema to many Americans. A part of our tradition says, "I'll do what I damn well please, and the rest of the world be damned!" That ethic, which abhors restraint of any kind, has indeed damned the world by trashing the environment at every self-indulgent turn. After striking and killing the doe, I began limiting my desire to drive whenever and wherever I wanted because I was more conscious of the impact that my automobile habit had on the natural world of Point Reyes. The death of the doe shocked me into seeing the consequences of using such an invasive contrivance as an automobile in such a sensitive and sentient world. Simply put, we must use cars with more awareness of the effect they have on the environment.

At around the same time, I took on a full-time job, with a tedious daily commute, as a counselor and case manager working with severely mentally ill clients—those with schizophrenia, major depression, and bipolar disorder, often coupled with and complicated by alcohol and drug addiction. Given my own history of having to cope with my anxiety disorder for so many years, I had tried to avoid stressful jobs, but I was a good counselor and a good listener and helper, and I was able to draw on my own experiences with mental illness to help others tack through rough waters.

In addition to writing, I had been providing counseling since the late '60s, but discovered that I could only function well for a period of time before feeling burned out. As a psychic astrologer once told me, it was as if I would insert a straw into the unconscious of a counseling client and but didn't know when to stop sipping. In other words, typical "boundary issues," as the mental health trade would say, a problem common to many professionals in the field who don't know how to draw the line when trying to help. To minimize the stress of that kind of work, and to allow myself time to write, I had usually worked part-time in settings that included prisons, hospitals, nursing homes, community outreach centers and mental health centers while writing freelance articles, essays, and books. The thought of doing full-time mental health counseling spiked my anxiety to uncomfortable levels, but my writing career was in the doldrums and I needed the money, so I took the job and the chance.

I began getting up before dawn so I could hike the trail each day to stay in shape and avoid my own mental meltdown. I knew I needed the trail for other reasons as well, especially for spiritual nourishment and renewal as I faced the intense suffering of clients with paranoia, delusions, hallucinations, anxiety, and depression. Medications controlled their symptoms to a degree but most were still scarred after years of self- (and society) inflicted stigma and abuse. The trail was as much a medicine for me as psychotropic medications were to those folks, and it had far fewer side effects. But side effects it had, especially in terms of its possibilities for bodily injuries.

More than any other time of day, the transition from night to day reminds us that we can start life anew each day, unburdened by the past if our mind chooses it so. Because so few humans are awake at this hour, the accumulated collective mental and emotional miasma of all those lives is more attenuated and subdued. This allows fresh thought to bubble up. Our body has not yet had to trundle around. Our day's busyness has not yet begun, so we can enjoy the respite of the transition between unconscious sleep and running around. And, though we may feel mentally sharp, we are often still too bleary-eyed to immediately start mustering the purpose, direction, and intention that will get the wheels of our "doing" spinning again for the coming day.

Unfortunately, my dawns were goal-oriented in that I had a strong desire to stay in shape while coping with my stressful full-time job. This led to a downfall. Without warming up sufficiently, I began hiking so vigorously in the pre-dawn cold (the job had begun at the start of the rainy winter season) that in a couple of months I started noticing an acute pain in my left knee, particularly in certain twisting positions on the downgrades. Although the pain kept increasing as spring came, I imagined that my legs were strong and impervious to any permanent damage, and I pushed away any thought that the problem could be more than a passing blip on my body's radar screen—nothing that couldn't be cured with more and harder exercise, using the standard American mantras of "push through it" and "no pain, no gain."

My first reaction to any bodily pain or discomfort, from a common cold to a paper cut, was usually denial. I didn't want to even admit a problem—a male syndrome in itself that a Zen master might have diagnosed as attachment to the body that could be cured only through a serious meditation practice. Because my ego was thoroughly identified with my body, any threat to my body's well-being alarmed my ego and aroused fear and chronic anxiety. This adversarial relationship with pain, a perfect setup for mental suffering, led to obsessive fear, anticipatory anxiety, and catastrophic thinking. So, as the weeks went on and sharp pain began accompanying almost every step, encountering the pain in my knee became like a personal interview with a spiritual master.

~

Pain as teacher....Pain as a prod forces us to go deeper into relationship with body, mind, spirit, and surrounding community and environment to find the cause and heal. A few months before, on a trip East to visit family, I drove my mother to the doctor for a supposedly routine procedure to tidy up an incision from an apparently successful triple bypass heart operation she'd had several weeks earlier. My anxiety about bodily suffering had dogged me since childhood, so I was already deep in the belly of that beast as the doctor started an archaic, though necessary (he assured us) procedure called debriding. As part of the operation, they had taken veins from my mother's legs. This had left an open, oozing wound that had been slow to heal. What the doctor did was start scraping the scar tissue from the area to prevent infection—but, for some skewed reason known only to himself and perhaps his shrink, he chose not to use any anesthesia. My mother cried out, reacting to pain more intense than anything I'd ever witnessed. I reassured her and stroked her back and prayed that he would soon finish. I began worrying that her heart might stop, and I asked the doctor about a local anesthetic, but he kept insisting that it wouldn't take much longer. He was rushed, he said, and was squeezing in this procedure between other operations, and anesthesia would take too long, he said, so it really would be just a few more minutes, he said. But Mother cried out each time his scalpel touched the open wound. I was scared for her. I felt like grabbing the knife and doing a little debriding on the doctor's throat...slowly.

It was the first time I had ever literally felt someone else's pain—and that this someone was my mother left a deep impression on me. This could have been the scene of my birth, and with each scrape of the scalpel, the pain of my mother's pushing and my struggle through the birth canal grew more intense. In the past, unable to face the anxiety associated with such pain, I might have fainted on the spot. But I surprised myself. What I did instead, that day, was to merge with my mother on a visceral level, which, without the mind to misinterpret and distort reality, may be the deepest layer of consciousness.

She surprised me, too. Here was this seemingly frail woman, 80-plus years old, enduring pain that would have made a battle-wounded soldier scream. All of life is view, say the Buddhists. Things are as each of us sees them, and that day I saw my mother in a new light. At once tough and vulnerable, she could respond to adversity—in this case, extreme pain—with grace and grit. In those moments, I learned more from her than I had in all the time I'd known her, and she hadn't said a word.

And when the "procedure" finally ended, she walked out of that office on her own steam—tottering, unsteady, but more elegant than a queen at her coronation.

Seeing my mother in pain, comforting her, and bonding with her changed my relationship with her—and with pain as well. As my knee condition worsened—it was eventually diagnosed as an inflammation of the bursa, a fluid-filled sac that facilitates motion between tendon and bone—my mind was able to ease around it and not scream so when the stun-gun pain would hit. Also, saying "the" mind instead of "my" mind helped me relate to pain as something universal, as something that connected me to all the pain that people were suffering, at that moment, throughout the universe. In *Who Dies?*, Stephen Levine called this the "experiencing of the personal in its universal aspect... The day I realized it wasn't my mind or my pain, but just the nature of the mind and pain itself, was an initiation that changed my relationship to pain forever. When it's 'the' pain, it has the whole universe to float in; when it's 'my' pain, I'm standing alone in it."

Worry—a family tradition—lingered, though. I added a walking stick to brace my descents and did daily leg lifts to strengthen the muscles around my kneecap. Even more importantly, for the first time in my life, I began to face my physical vulnerability, and, by extension, my mortality. From age, wear, and trauma, a part of my body had failed, limiting an activity I had written books about, linked part of my livelihood to, built a persona upon, and derived part of life's meaning through. In the biographical note for my first book, a walking and historical guide to the San Francisco Bay area, I had defined myself both as writer and walker. What would I be, what would life be like, if I could not walk? What if I were bedridden? Would life be worth living?

Every time the sharp pain struck, those questions arose. As my mother had shown me, it wasn't so much pain itself that was the problem as my relationship to it. Pain is a reminder of the true nature of the body. From the moment we are born, the body ages, decays, and eventually dies. Buddhist monks have a practice where they spend hours watching a corpse as it decays so they will be less attached to the body and more connected to that True Nature that never dies or breaks down. Our eternal True Soul only requires acknowledgment, every day, every hour, every moment. Without pain, death, and decay to remind us that all things in the universe are impermanent, as the Buddhists say, we might forsake our need to break the conditioning of fear that links our sense of ourselves with the fate of our bodies.

"So pain is good?" asks a wiseguy part of myself.

"Well, not exactly good," the eternal me answers, "but valuable in the overall scheme of things."

"You're talking overall scheme—I'm talking pain in the knee. How about a pill or something?"

The inner dialogue: Will it never cease? Will the part that wants things otherwise never be content with what is? We certainly needn't desire to be in pain, and when it arises, it's fine to do whatever we can to make it go away. But before we take the pill or have the surgery, we might want to look closely at our relationship to pain and how we might learn from it.

Pain can teach us about how we are living our lives on physical, emotional, and spiritual levels. For the most part, our minds are negatively conditioned by pain, and our relationship to it is adversarial. When it comes, we want it gone—fast. At the beginning of one Sasaki Roshi-led Zen meditation retreat, while I was sitting in a very uncomfortable cross-legged position, I suddenly had the feeling of a knife sticking into the middle of my back. The pain was intense, and I wanted it away. It was disturbing my peace and tranquility, I thought at the time. But I knew something of Zen practice and so I continued watching, feeling, and being with that pain for three days. There was nothing to do about it, no pills to take, no doctors to see, just to sit still and experience that pain. As I did so, the pain stopped being an enemy and started to be just what it was in the moments it was there. At the middle of the third day, it left as suddenly as it had come. I never felt it again during that retreat, and I also experienced the deepest calm, and even bliss, that I had ever felt, not because the pain had left but because I had sat with it, had gotten to know and accept it, and had stopped resisting and judging it as something undesirable. I had broken a pattern of conditioning, and I knew that I didn't have to be as afraid of pain as I had been before. By not continually wishing the pain away, I had created the possibility of entering into a more dynamic, creative relationship with it.

Over time, the knee pain I felt when hiking became more sporadic. From then on, though, I practiced an increased awareness of how and where I placed my feet. I watched more for loose rocks and exposed roots and places where water-carved mini-canyons could catch the edge of my boot in case my eyes were entranced by a seductive hawk, a patch of wildflowers, or an orb web bejeweled with morning dew. I became more attentive to the nuances of sensation in my knee, to the little creaks and pops I had grossly categorized before as pain. But pain seen closely has degrees, signals, barometers, precursors, and harbingers. As with thoughts, if I catch the warning signs early, I can watch my reactions more closely and prevent the mind from detonating the dynamite of fear. I can relax and soften around it and thus prevent muscles from tightening, bracing, and ultimately, perhaps, snapping under the strain. I can slow my pace, modify the length of my step, change my posture, carry a stick, avoid uneven areas and loose rocks on downhill terrain, attend to where I place my feet on the up-slopes, and wear boots with good tread.

Pain as blessing? I don't seek or welcome it, but when it comes, it focuses my attention. It forces a closer look at the important minutiae of moving, thinking, acting, talking, and working as it constantly instructs me where to make adjustments and changes in the gears of living. Again, nature is the model. Several years after the Point Reyes fire, the understory is alive with new growth. New plants are taking advantage of the new soil environment. A new generation of Bishop pine saplings is vibrant and healthy. Birds are back, as are deer in greater numbers. Small rodents are proliferating, which keeps the hawks, kites, and owls happy. Coyotes howl with joy at the mice and rabbits and are returning to the area. Elk are now foraging in the fire-scarred areas to the west and south of Sky Trail and Inverness Ridge. Even a black bear, perhaps drawn to the area's abundance, has apparently migrated south from Sonoma County. The forest is continually adjusting, adapting, and responding to Teacher Pain and doing what it does so well—grow. We might do well to follow Teacher Forest.

EXPLORING YOUR PATH

> What is your relationship to physical pain? A headache? A morning backache? A head cold? A diagnosis of high blood pressure? Prostate cancer? This isn't a question with a right or wrong answer. It's just an invitation for you to bring awareness to your reactions when you experience pain. Take a few minutes to write in your journal, and consider this entry a baseline. Over the next week, continue to monitor your reactions to and thoughts about pain and record them in your journal.

> What is your relationship to emotional pain? Fear and anxiety? Sadness? Depression? Frustration? Rejection? Disappointment? Abandonment? Anger? Do you rush to medicate? Do you take time to be with and understand what is happening? Is emotional upset ever a teacher for you? Again, take time to reflect on these questions and to write about them in your journal.

> The next time you feel physical or emotional pain, go to a soul place in nature and take a walk with that pain. Go slowly, because pain needs time to explain itself. Talk with it. Put your critical, judgmental mind aside and try to understand pain's message. When you return home, take a few minutes to write in your journal about any insights you gained.

Wind-ing

During the El Nino winter of 1997-98, great storms battered the peninsula. One of my favorite things was to don raingear, head to toe, and, following the lead of the great naturalist John Muir, walk in storms—the stronger the better—putting myself at more risk than I usually do on an average day. As a youngster, I had loved reading sailing adventure novels, complete with harrowing storms and how the hero rode them out. I loved East Coast winter storms, too, with their wild winds and drifting snows.

So when I heard about a terrific storm massing in the Pacific just off the coast, I covered myself in raincoat, rainpants, and waterproof boots, and headed out in search of the heart of a storm on Sky Trail. Of course, here in northern coastal California, it isn't snow that's the headliner but rain and wind. Wind and water are the great sculptors of the coastline—chiseling cliffs, sculpting beaches and dunes, carving inlets and estuaries, shaping trees more expertly than a bonsai master.

Wind especially is the Merlin of nature. You can see its work—trees straining, sand blowing, objects swirling, cliffs carved—but you can't actually see it working, as you can rain, snow, or hail. Like breath, it is divine *spiritus*—subtle at times, irregular and choppy at others, but, for the most part, at Point Reyes anyway, nearly constant. Whether blustery or balmy, wind is neither good nor bad. It is "wind"-ing, one of the natural activities of a universe where subject and object are one. The noun is also its own verb, making the actions of the universe genuine, complete unto themselves, fully realized and free. Such is wind.

~

This day, it is not only blowing freely but especially hard. I flash on the image of a tree limb falling upon me. The anticipatory thought severs my involvement with the present. Programmed to respond to certain cues with fear and catastrophic thinking, I am again separate from nature. And again I realize that I make up the world around me. That is to say, I make up my attitude about the world, and that attitude becomes my concept of the world, instead of my experiencing the world itself. Without the human mind to interpret it, the world itself, is without attitude or view or perception. The world itself, the natural world, including its elements, flora, and fauna, simply exists, untouched by opinions, fears, and projections. Nature is all verb, and verbs, like pure Bill Haley and the Comets, shake, rattle, rock, and roll.

At first I walk slowly, seasoning myself to the volatile storm. Familiar trees and bushes thrash about like mad monkeys. None of the usual deer, brush rabbits, sparrows, stink beetles, fence lizards are about. Everyone is holed up in burrows, nests, caves, under rocks, wherever, hoping to ride out this unusually powerful storm.

Everyone except me.

It is mid-afternoon, but as dark as dusk. Fir and pine, tow-ering tall and foreboding in their long, evergreen capes, sway like ghouls in a Halloween horror movie. I wonder if their roots grab hold of the soil more tenaciously in such wind and send messages to the rest of the tree, to each cell in each leaf: "Hold on! Brace yourself!" When any aspect of nature, in this case wind, goes to extremes, all the rest react in protective ways to ensure survival. I alone, being where trees could fall and boulders could roll, am out looking for drama, adventure, and perhaps some danger—that Faustian dance with death that only humans know and act upon.

Not long before, I had opened my heart to a woman whose long marriage had recently ended. She was willing and inter-ested, but ultimately the timing was wrong. We had known each other before and liked each other very much. A relationship seemed a natural next step. Sadly, she wasn't ready. I turned inward to lick my wounds, which is where walking in a violent storm on the razor's edge between rational and irrational behav-ior comes in. The strong, raw wind exposes my vulnerability and makes it easier for me to turn my wounds over to nature for healing. The visceral, violent storm cuts through my habit-ual cerebro-centrism and brings me face to face with my core feelings.

As the wind whips and swirls with increasing ferocity, I hear old dead trees crack and moan and fall. Only once before, dur-ing the silence of a meditation retreat at a remote monastery in northern California, had I seen a tree fall, and it did indeed make a noise—a mighty crack and thud like a cymbal and ket-tledrum ending a symphony. It was as if the tree fell into my ear, merging observer and observed, hearing and hearer. In that instant, nothing separated the tree and me, for the tree and my hearing the tree fall were the same.

Such is the mechanism of healing. When the doors of my senses open, unfiltered by judgment or discrimination, I am more at peace with myself and my immediate environment. As I embraced the sound of that falling tree on the monastery grounds, I renewed my membership in Gaia, the planet alive.

Along with sound, other sense doors open. I take in the smells of the storm, the salt-sea air, the sap from broken tree limbs, soil soaked and musty, the primal odors of moss and mushrooms seeping from the forest floor. A deep, green, ripened by rain, variegated in shades and hues and textures, as radiant as a young bride, floods the landscape and my eyes. Green is as ancient as Earth. It is the color of my soul and connects me with all green everywhere. I walk up toward the summit, green to my core, and imagining God not as the white-bearded ancient of the Bible but as an amorphous mass, dripping and oozing green through and through.

The wind gusts to what feels like hurricane force. I lean into it as a hard rain drives against my face. Though cloaked in nylon, I am still damp, because rain of such intensity infiltrates seams down through cotton to skin, until "soaked to the bone" borders on reality. This wildness of wind touches that part of me that so rarely surfaces in day-to-day life, where the closest most of us get to wildness is putting out a flare-up in our backyard barbecue. But inner wildness exists alongside the sacred, and the storm heightens that awareness. In that moment, nature seems violent, out of control, and yet, ultimately, as destructive as the storm was, it too grows the forest and, by extension, all life. My own stormy feelings—anger, grief, fear—those gut sensations that defy rationality, push and coerce me to look at life more honestly. They refuse sequestration. They refuse containment. They refuse the brush-off. They will be heard, whether through hair loss or headache, ulcer or allergy, cancer or a cold, impotence or infection. They will refuse to go unheard, and, once heard, will grow my soul.

Pushing through the wall of wind to the summit of Wittenberg, I again dance the Tai Chi. I feel as if the northwest wind may lift me and blow me across the Olema Valley to the huge hump of Elephant Mountain to the east. I continue the graceful Cloud Hands for a long time, in a trance of emptying and becoming, of dancing and being danced by the storm. Hard rain, a strong squall line, begins pelting and pushing, and the sky blackens and the wind hits the ridge like a charging fullback. I stop my dance and brace my body against the force of the weather, I feel alive and awakened to something wild within, something that has no bounds, and we are not easy with things that have no bounds.

We have tried to tame and control the boundless world by inventing the lines of longitude and latitude, the lines that separate nation states, the defining lines of the road, and the lines that create parcels of "private" property. We see neat, orderly weather maps announced by neat, orderly weather forecasters dressed impeccably, with neat, orderly hair. Have they not been out in the wind all day? Have they not been drenched by the rain they are reporting on? Have they no mud on their shoes? They create the illusion that everything is under control, that this weather is just a thing that the computer is modeling, or that radar is tracking, or that satellites are monitoring. And we the viewers are lulled into believing that because the weather is reportable, it is controllable. We feel safe watching the weather on TV, as if hearing it described and illustrated takes away some of its power. We give its wild elements labels—highs and lows, split jet streams, temperature inversions, tropical moisture, and cold fronts. The weather becomes merely the next scheduled show, and we tune into Storm Watch as much for entertainment as for real practical information.

The terrific storm I have chosen to experience has no lines to define and predict it. For all the TV weather I have watched, I find that I cannot think about this storm in rational terms. It telegraphs raw energy, and the first message that hits my brain is fear. The storm strikes with a ferocity that would have scared Zeus himself. Coyote brush and small trees seem to strain to hold their roots. And I feel that if I put out my arms in Cloud Hands, the wind might pick me up and fling me inland several miles into someone's back yard.

A sudden series of mighty, spasmodic gusts hits the ridge like rockets—a final barrage, for soon the wind weakens to strong breezes and a glaze of rain.

~

My ancient dance continues—the Creeping Snake, the Golden Rooster on One Leg, Punch and Parry, Searching for a Needle at the Bottom of the Sea, again Repulsing the Monkey—and finally, sweeping my hands down to the ground, I lift the *anima mundi*—the soul of the world—and set it down on Earth as I would a crystal heirloom.

Then I descend the trail, no longer as burdened by the raw emotions that drew me out to the storm. All things arise and pass away, says Ajahn Sumedho, reminding us of this central teaching of the Buddha. I see this truth evidenced firsthand in this intense wind and rain storm, which is now whimpering away. And, like the storm, difficult emotions do not last forever. They pass, and in their passing they renew our capacity for regeneration and restore our faith that we can deal with just about anything if we honor the natural ebb and flow of life.

EXPLORING YOUR PATH

> The next chance you get, take a walk in some weather, preferably on your soul trail. Feel the wind, rain, or snow on your face. Walk with the wind. Walk against it. Get wet. Feel cold. Seek out mud puddles. Go home and get warm. Have some tea. Sit in a nice easy chair and smile a bit at letting yourself go wild for a while.

> Did the weather frighten you? Exhilarate you? Numb you? Surprise you? Overwhelm you? Excite you? Enchant you? Hook you? What do you feel after the experience? How did the experience affect your relationship with your soul trail? Take a few minutes to write about what you're thinking and feeling.

> Reflect on any past experiences you may have had with severe weather. Was this experience different? In what ways?

Spring Eternal

CHAPTER 15

Signs of spring can arrive as early as February in northern California. As a former New Englander, I used to find this unsettling, but now my Northeast-bred bones welcome and settle into the lovely early warmth. New flowers, grasses, buds, blossoms, colors, textures, smells, all woven together, began to dance their tarantella in the gusty wind. Winter provided the landscape with a deep green background wash ready for the finer, color brushes of spring.

On the trail, sometimes as early as late February, the first color comes from the Douglas irises, the color of the sky with a dab of deep purple, and the delicate baby blue-eyes, robin's-egg blue on clusters of slender stems that look like skinny, giggling prep-school girls. Forget-me-nots soon follow. Liking the shade of the fir forest, they weave themselves together in a lace of light blue. Although botanists consider them no more than a weed that has blown to the wild from town gardens, to my eyes they resemble an embroidered fringe of ground cover, each one as meticulously painted as a print on a summer dress. In March, the California poppy, the famous state flower that even a New Englander recognizes, begins to bud and unfurl and glow a satiny orange, growing low to counter the unremitting vernal northwest winds. By early April, the California huckleberry, its thick, shining, dark-green leaves so striking that poachers fence them to florists, starts showing its flowers, which look like tiny pink Chinese lanterns bobbing on a string. By then, single stems of blue-eyed grass, a cousin of the iris, are also somehow standing tall in the stiff ridge-top breezes.

The winds of spring—generated, scientists tell us, by the clash of high barometric pressure offshore and low pressure in California's Central Valley—whip through and around my spirit like a genie granting wishes I haven't even made yet and push me out and beyond the confines erected by the hermit winter. The winds are the verbs of spring—active, alive, moving life along with a force greater, at times, than breath. I imagine that love blew the universe into being with its breath, a wind so great that matter shattered into planets and suns and solar systems, that waters parted from land and clouds parted from water, a wind so powerful that it formed life and filled it with the breath of love.

The spring wind, sometimes gusting to 80 miles per hour but averaging 35, inspires me to flight. In my mind's eye, I soar with the osprey, the red-tailed hawk, the American kestrel, the black-shouldered kite. I dive and dart with violet-green swallows and purple martins, white-crowned sparrows, wrentits, and the gorgeous green and red flashes of Anna's hummingbirds. I grab the wings of a willing osprey and ride the air currents effortlessly over ridge and sea. Borrowing its eyes, I can see California gray whales migrating north from their spawning bays in Baja California, newts embraced in sexual ecstasy in quiet pools of woodland streams, the gray fox, the bobcat, and now—more protected from poisons and hunting—the coyote, that trickster, gamboling through high-grass meadows and stalking prey. Tule elk graze just west of Inverness Ridge, and deer gorge themselves on new clover and wild rye. The osprey whistles its clear, high call, sets me down gently, and flaps its five-foot wingspan deep and slow as it ascends to check its nest and feed its fledglings high in the dead branches of a firmly standing fir not far from the trailhead.

Spring on the trail is an elixir that heals everything lethargic and woebegone in my psyche. From the ubiquitous wind to the territorial calls of migratory songbirds returning to northern exposures to the screaming serenade of Jerusalem crickets in the meadows near the trail, I am lifted above any personal story that may be dragging me down. Spring seems to linger past the June solstice, and the wildflower show continues despite the increasing summer fog. The bright-yellow footsteps of spring, a personal favorite, are gone by, as is the iris, but the Peter-Max-pop-orange poppy flourishes still, and the hardy Indian paintbrush brightens brushy areas with its striking reds.

Spring makes it easy to stay present with life, to celebrate simple moments, to live, as Jesus suggested in the Sermon on the Mount, like the "lilies of the field" in raiment more lavish than "even Solomon in all his glory," not for the morrow but for today, amid spring's display.

~

Passion abounds. I remember the time I strayed off-trail and a Northern harrier hawk attacked me on six separate dives. I had apparently come too close to its nest, usually located in tall grasses on the ground or in marshy areas (which accounts for its common name of marsh hawk). I had seen this deft hunter fly-ing just a few feet off the ground before, but never when I was the hunted. The eyes of that threatened and threatening raptor at two feet above my head were fiercer and more alive than any eyes I'd ever seen. Determined in flight and purpose, he was a being totally being itself. No doubts. No decisions to make. No anger. No retribution. Just a hawk acting to protect its young. As I dodged each dive and pass, I completely understood the depth of the hawk's commitment and mission.

From my perspective, I was just passing through, without harm-ful intent, but to the hawk, I was a threat. It had no way of know-ing how progressive an environmentalist I fancied myself to be or how pure my motives were. I hurried away, and the hawk ended its sorties. I wondered afterwards whether I could live and act that completely, that sincerely—with thought, instinct, action, and spirit harmonized as one. My life often seems a series of spasms—one action followed by reaction followed by action. If lucky, I reach my destination, but drained of that unified and unifying Hawk Spirit.

How different are our two lives, I reflected. The hawk lives and works and plays not in what humans define as a "habitat" but in a place occupied by hawks for eons. Conditions change with fire, drought, earthquake, and human machinations, but the hawk adapts, sometimes pulling back, sometimes attacking, remembering points of danger, but never dissipating energy, as I do in my mulling, pondering, fretting, doubting. The hawk nav-igates obstacles and satisfies its needs with minimal impact on the sensitive landscape. The hawk is not merely a survivor but an artist that shapes its world with its wings and leaves no tracks.

I, less an artist than the hawk, leave tracks. I drive a car that requires carving a road through ancient migration routes. As the doe I killed showed, the road and my car have transformed the landscape into a game of Russian roulette where the next car can be a bringer of death.

Earth is safer in the hands of this hawk than it is in mine. Human adaptation charges ahead and shapes and manipulates. The hawk takes only what it needs and leaves the rest unharmed. It acts, and Earth, undisturbed, continues its quotidian embrace of all and everything—of hunger, satisfaction, fear, peace, abundance, breath, day, night, rain, drought, fire, birth, death, mating, play. But, according to a 2003 article in the journal *Nature*, we humans have pushed our life-giving planet to the point where, due to global warming, nearly a quarter of all land-based plant and animal species on Earth could become extinct in just a few decades. When we humans act, Earth gasps and must brace itself against our insensitivity and unwillingness to accommodate and sacrifice for the sake of the planet's health.

~

The hawk, resuming its search for voles, shrews, and mice to feed its brood, ascends to scan the terrain. At the deepest core of our being, we are the same, that hawk and I. Perhaps the more superficial parts of me will one day molt like a snake's skin, and I'll meld with the artistry of that hawk, which lives love with every breath, every dive for prey, every salvo past an interloper's head.

EXPLORING YOUR PATH

> What are the signs of spring on or near your soul trail? Do you notice weather changes? New plants? More animal activity? New colors?

> What does spring do to you—to your body, mind, and spirit?

> Honor not only spring, but also the beginning of every new season. Create your own rituals. These might include a ceremonial walk, a breaking of bread, a flinging of stones into water, a canoe trip, a silent meditation on a mountaintop. You decide. Write or draw your ritual in your journal.

Letting Go

CHAPTER 16

Spring enticed me to leave the safety of the trail after the wet, muddy winterand notch up the hiking risk factor by doing some scrambling. I was bushwhacking, exploring off-trail in a brushy, rocky section, when I reached up to grab a branch to hoist myself higher. The branch seemed strong and pliant, but I wondered if it was thick enough to bear my weight. I flashed back on an episode years before in Yosemite when a branch I was trying to break for kindling resisted and finally snapped as I jumped to use my body weight to break it off. I fell hard and injured my back severely, which I thought had made me learn my lesson. This time, I again decided to grab onto the branch. It bent beyond a point that looked safe, and I knew I should let it go, but I didn't. Instead, I chose once more to put my mind, via my hand, into a monkey trap of suffering.

South American monkey hunters use a simple, effective device to capture monkeys alive so they can sell them on the zoo, pet, and research markets. The hunters tether a gourd to a tree, widen one end slightly, and bait it with a chunk of food big enough to fit in the gourd without falling out. The monkey comes along, smells the food, puts its hand in the gourd, grabs the food, and tries to pull its fist out so it can eat the food. But the hole is too small for the monkey to pull out its hand unless it lets go of the food. The monkey won't let go, and all the hunter has to do is slip the captured monkey into his sack.

Why doesn't the monkey just open its fist, let go of the food, pull out its hand, and escape? Why, indeed? Because the monkey has only one thing in mind—the food in its hand—and it refuses to let go even as the hunter approaches. The trap is actually not the gourd, but the monkey's own mind, fueled by its desires and attachment to the food in its hand.

In that moment when the branch bowed so dangerously, all I (slightly more advanced monkey that I am) had to do was let go of it, let go of my stubborn determination (a form of greed, really), and all would have been as it was before. That is, I would have gone on scrambling about in the bush uninjured. But I held on and pulled, and the branch cracked, and I fell back, slammed my shoulder hard against a tree behind me, and tumbled to the ground. "Pain hurts," as a five-year-old once told me.

How many more times in this life will I reach into the trap, grab the figurative food, refuse to let go, and incarcerate myself yet again in a prison of my own making? How many more times will I chant that after-the-fact mantra, "I knew I shouldn't have done that"? Once, at a meditation retreat in rural northern California, I was walking across a pasture when I came upon a lamb that had wedged its head in a fence—a bad move on the lamb's part because it would soon have become dinner for the nearby vultures. I freed it and it gamboled off. But I puzzle over the fact that, although my brain is considerably more advanced than that lamb's, my own entrapments involve the same mental processes. Why do I, with millennia of cerebral cortex development, do such things? Am I not a free man? Am I not in control of my self, my mind?

At the moment I clutched at the bent branch, an inner wisdom told me that I should let go and be at peace. But my ego shouted down that wisdom. I can do it, I thought. I won't be hurt. The branch will hold and I will be able to pull myself up. I will. I will. I will.

"I will."

Over the centuries, "I will" has created much. "I will" created both the frescoes in the Sistine Chapel and the depletion of the ozone layer. "I will" invented both indoor plumbing and shopping malls built on filled-in wetlands. "I will" resulted in the moon landing in 1969, and 30 years earlier, the start of WWII. My own "I will" has let me counsel and help hundreds of people and to write books and articles—but it cannot free me from the monkey trap of my mind. In fact, it is that "I will" that gets me into the trap in the first place, no matter how much I try to shift the responsibility to my parents or teachers or society, or even God. So, too, the way out is also completely up to me.

If I could just open my hand and let go...of all I imagined I needed to be happy...of wanting everything to go my way...of my ideas of life...of self and will...of branches—real and figurative—that seem strong enough. To let go in the knowledge that I don't need any of these to be a full, alive, realized human being.

~

Fortunately, my fall wasn't serious. I got up and even continued my bushwhacking to the top of Mount Wittenberg. I was lucky, I guess. I found myself reflecting that the world, too, has been lucky since human beings have gotten their paws on weapons that can destroy the planet—weapons that we can't seem to let go of because "I will," with all its greed, hatred, and delusion, continues to dominate dealings between people and nations. Will that "I will" eventually lead us to put our hand into one monkey trap too many?

As for my own personal traps, I'm sure that many more, all baited with things I want, lie ahead. I know that I will wobble, again and again, at the edge of a consciousness that would require only that I open my eyes and hands to be free.

EXPLORING YOUR PATH

> Make an inventory of your attachments—those things
> you have or would have particular difficulty letting go
> of if you needed to. These things are addictions if the
> clinging corrodes your and your family's health and
> well-being, or the letting go feels impossible. What
> branches do you hold on to even when it is obvious
> that you should let go? What do you refuse to let go
> of even when you see its negative effects? With as
> much honesty as you can muster, and remembering
> that no one else need see what you write, make an
> inventory in your journal.

> Becoming aware of attachments is the first step toward ridding ourselves of them and bringing freedom of choice back into our life. The exercise above was designed to help you see. Now, begin to experiment with letting go of harmful attachments. But here's the beautiful paradox—the very acts of seeing and experiencing our attachments are a letting-go, because we don't usually see them at all. Instead, we are usually lost in them, the same way that at one moment we might pass a bakery and then suddenly find ourselves shoving an éclair into our mouth. When you become aware, you shine light on the problem, and problems usually thrive only in the darkness of our minds. This light can also be called being honest with yourself, and honesty, in its fullest forms, is a step along the path of smashing the shackles of attachment and addiction. But don't believe what I say, as Ajahn Sumedho would say: Try it for yourself, and write about it.

Soul Home

Air is warm, fog is rare, in the early fall, and as I stand atop Mount Wittenberg—my own Mount Olympus—I look out to an ocean and headlands made impressionistic by the filtered light that adds pastel hues to the already soft landscape. Autumnal winds blow strongly at times but not with the constancy of the vernals. After no appreciable rain in six months, the possibility of fire coupled with big winds, as happened in 1995, is always a worry. Birds of prey soar down the valleys, deer lounge on the ridge's open, grassy meadows, bucks joust for the rut. Wittenberg's summit is covered with firs the size of Christmas trees stunted by the weather. They sway and bend in the breeze, but without bracing and holding on as they would in a violent squall or winter storm.

Mesmerized by the magical light, somehow milky and clear at the same time, I lose all sense of time and even all sense of self-watching. This place, which I feel has been my soul home throughout and before time, unfurls into fullness like a maple-leaf bud. Every thing in the landscape—every blade of grass, wildflower, jackrabbit, doe, vulture, sparrow, beetle—is familiar, is family, in that flick of timelessness. Everything dances—that purest of art forms that leaves no prints, no record of its performance. I can't even say whether the scene before me is real and alive. I've lost my frame of reference, and without it I can't even say if I am alive. I simply am. "I am that I am," the God of the Old Testament told Moses. So, in that moment (and I can't even call it a moment, for "moment" is by definition a measure of time), I (and I can't even say "I," for I have no sense of being separate from anything that might be other than I) am part of the timeless, "the Deathless," as Ajahn Sumedho calls it. The future, the past, and even the present are gone. Eyes, ears, nose, tongue, body gone, as the Buddhist Heart Sutra teaches. Mind gone. A place where life is simply lived, without remorse or doubt. Such a place, being a good place to live, is an equally good place to die.

In that blessed state, I am immersed in bliss, immersed in "I am that I am." All around is love, not love as I have come to know it or was taught, but love that cares for and embraces all life always. Even purpose disappears. Life itself is enough. "I am sufficient as I am," wrote Walt Whitman, content with nothing other than life's brocade. Love is a cocoon, and if I could metamorphose and allow it to embrace me as it has forever, I could emerge a liberated butterfly—that essence of joy that flips and dips and flutters and sips, living only a short time but offering a glimpse of eternity. But as I twist to get a better stance, a sharp pain stings my knee and rekindles the embers of aversion and fear, and out of the cocoon I tumble, still a caterpillar.

A caterpillar again, yes, but every time love enters and blossoms in my heart, another piece of the love puzzle finds its place. Like each brush stroke as an artist creates a painting, the picture begins to form—a love picture that we know intimately, that we saw and felt as infants. Love. Unconditional love. The puzzle was complete. Then, as we grew up, the puzzle was overturned. Pieces scattered. Some were lost. Some we found again, but we couldn't figure out where they fit. So some of us went to religion or psychotherapy or spiritual practice to look for the pieces of love and reconstruct the puzzle. Some of us didn't look at all but merely reduced our daily life to financial, physical, emotional, mental, and spiritual survival. Eventually, though, we will all have more chances as the wheel of life and death continues to turn. And someday we will learn that enlightenment or satori or liberation or sainthood or a gracefull life means getting all the pieces of love back and literally falling in love with the universe again, as we did viscerally when we were infants.

It's not easy, recovering the pieces of the puzzle. In our culture, even the word "love" is misunderstood and distorted. "Some Buddhist teachers prefer 'loving-kindness,' as they find the word 'love' too dangerous," Thich Nhat Hanh once said in a newspaper interview. "Words sometimes get sick and we have to heal them. We have been using the word 'love' to mean appetite or desire, as in 'I love hamburgers.' We have to use language more carefully. We have to restore the meaning of the word love. 'Love' is a beautiful word. We have to restore its meaning..."

And yet we have stripped it of meaning by trying to ascribe meaning to it. Love is what the whole universe is made of and to describe it may be to risk losing it, as has happened only too often. Loving the trail, I come here. I walk. I feel. I talk. I laugh. I cry. My mind quiets. It babbles. It rests in eternity, even if just for a moment. In eternity, I am in love. In eternity, I am in life.

But, humans that we are, we can't just leave it there in the sweet ether of

not-knowing, can we? We must invoke God or Jesus or Buddha or Allah or the Great Spirit. We must name that which needs no name. We must lasso love, corral it, tame it, name it, and ride it, curb its wild temper, subdue it so we can "understand" it, label it, categorize it. To what family, genus, and species does love belong? When will it appear next? What will it look like? Will it act as we expect it to? Love has become yet another product, packaged and promoted to gain maximum "market share." "The word is so loaded and corrupted that I hardly like to use it," wrote Krishnamurti in his essay "On Love." "Is love an idea? If it is, it can be cultivated, nourished, cherished, pushed around, twisted in any way you like."

Love is not an idea. This ground I stand on, the clouds, the headlands across Drake's Bay, the Pacific Ocean, the trees around me—all these may be ideas, may be things I make up and try to solidify by attaching labels to them that create an illusion of reality. But, despite perceptions and interpretations, love is no illusion. Though it cannot be held and possessed, love is real and boundless. Love is eternal, and anything eternal is beyond the mind's lines of latitude and longitude. Love exists in the realm of heart and soul. It cannot be created or extinguished. It always was and always will be, even if, five billion years from now, as astronomers warn us, our sun goes supernova, even if a black hole swallows our galaxy. Even after our bodies and our separate identities die, the love that was in us will continue its song and dance. No need to worry about it ending. It won't.

Love, as the original element of the universe, is crazy, irrational, full of so much passion that it fuels everything down to the smallest cell. Love is Emerson's fine madman in the wood, as he wrote in his essay "Love" in *Essays*, "…a palace of sweet sounds and sights; he dilates; he is twice a man; he walks with arms akimbo; he soliloquizes; he accosts the grass and the trees; he feels the blood of the violet, the clover and the lily in his veins; and he talks with the brook that wets his foot." Love is Lewis Carroll's "beamish boy" in his proud father's arms on the "frabjous day" that the boy slew the Jabberwock. Love is Krishnamurti's "innocent mind"—that which is new, fresh, alive. It has no yesterday and no tomorrow. It lies beyond the turmoil of thought. "True love," wrote Sasaki Roshi in *Buddha Is the Center of Gravity*, "does not belong to the world of language."

Love respects no boundaries. It rides roughshod over our most carefully made plans and challenges our rigid, calcified views, opinions, and perspectives. Sometimes love spills over into romantic love and creates situations we haven't foreseen or bargained on. Example: A few years ago, I fell in love with a woman who lived in a country almost halfway around the world. Go figure. I wanted to find someone in my neighborhood, but love, from my limited perspective, didn't get the target right. Still, after meeting her and walking Sky Trail together one late summer day, I saw my soul home in new, fresh ways— soft beams of light filtering through the Douglas fir forest in the receding fog; wild plants I had never noticed before, like the tall, elegant pearly everlasting, a cousin of edelweiss, the minty yerba buena; and the exhilaration of my first time on the trail as I relived it that day through Ruth's eyes. In June 2001, Ruth and I married, and we continue hiking these coastal hills with the spirit and perspective of beginners.

Holding my wife's hand, I begin experiencing the ridge top in new ways. No longer rooted in time or language, its expression of itself is itself. It is "summit-ing." And dancing. And so, too, am I. In some moments, I am no longer Stephen Altschuler, writer, counselor, walker, man. I am dancing, and I could take that as my name—I Am Dancing. I am not consciously "in love" with this hill, this trail, this forest, for that would be to objectify them. I-am-that-I-am-dancing, and with dancing there is no subject tracked or object danced.

~

Here, then, would be a good place to die—a place where I couldn't define myself as anything I had ever known, a place that knew me better than I knew me. It is a blessing to find a good place to die. I couldn't look for it. I couldn't try to locate it. I couldn't make a list of its characteristics. I couldn't repeat affirmations hoping to clear away the barriers to its discovery. But to live this life fully, I had to find it. I had to settle my mind accounts there and come to some sort of peace. I had to find the place where I could face myself squarely, honestly, courageously.

A good place to die is not a place at all. It is a state of mind. Krishnamurti said that simplifying one's life has little to do with reducing possessions or driving less or eating only vegetables. It is more a matter of our thoughts, and how much they busy and trouble the mind. When grace comes and the mind quiets, that is a good time and place to die—not necessarily the death of the body, although that will come, and where it happens is a consideration, but the cessation of all thought that separates the self from that state of being beyond birth and death. And when thought stills, love appears—simply, expressively, as a flower, a pinecone, a salamander, a blade of grass, a sparrow, a bull elk, a cloud, a mountain, a loon, a dandelion seed ball, a woman from halfway around the world.

~

As if I were walking with an unselfconscious five-year-old, I descend the summit slowly. Dead to the world of opposing thought, can I maintain this aliveness? Dead to images of myself, can I leave my footsteps behind, as a dancer does? Dead to doubt, can I forever entrust my soul to its keepers?

I reach the trailhead, turn, bow deeply to Sky Trail, and reclaim, with deep gratitude and reverence, another piece of the love puzzle. "Only that day dawns to which we are awake," Thoreau wrote in the last paragraph of *Walden*. Awake, I pray that my Cloud Hands will touch another day that dawns on this journey home.

EXPLORING YOUR PATH

> Reflect on your own love puzzle. What pieces still need to be reclaimed and healed? Whom do you need to forgive? What do you need to let go of? What thoughts still trigger emotional pain? Can you write about this in your journal?

> Go to your trail with this new information about your love puzzle. Walk slowly and let the trail alone help heal what needs to be healed.

> If you were to die today, and you knew this and had time to reflect upon your life, would you have any regrets, any particularly fond memories, any decisions you would rejoice over, any things of importance you have learned during your life, any things about yourself you would change, anyone you need to talk to but have avoided up to now, any internal issues you need to acknowledge and face, any amends to make, any thanks to express, any tears to cry or laughs to laugh or sense doors to open? Anything to let go of? Buy a new pen with just the right feel, find a comfortable spot in your home or in nature, and record your thoughts in your journal.

> And suppose you had another day? Week? Month? Year?...

EPILOGUE / BENEDICTION

My home is now about an hour's drive from the trail, so I don't get to hike there as often as before. I miss its quiet ways and how it could soothe me on the most hectic of days after my two-freeway commute into Oakland. Now I go sporadically, a pilgrim returning to re-charge, to re-mind and re-heart and re-soul myself with what is most important in this fleeting life. Because I don't go there as often, I am no longer as connected to its cycles. I see fewer mammals and birds. I pick fewer huckleberries. I photograph fewer flowers. I walk less in the moonlight.

Still, Sky Trail remains alive within. I carry with me my own private Sky Trail. Although it is an actual place in time and space, it is more. This place does not belong to me, but rather belongs "in" me, and "of" me – a soul home, a place I can retreat to whenever I wish just by directing my thoughts and imagining its richness. I am wealthy with a half-dozen soul homes— my long-ago New Hampshire cabin, a winter beach retreat on outer Cape Cod, a Buddhist monastery south of London, another atop Mount Baldy near Los Angeles.... Increasingly, though, I can quiet my mind and find my soul homes without imagining any external place, for a soul home is not so much a place as a state of mind and spirit – it is a Path.

Part of what I hoped to convey in this book is that we take care of what we love. Our Earth is in need of care. Generally governments and most citizens have a cavalier attitude towards nature. We use it, we play in it, we admire it, we exploit it, we talk about it, we enjoy it, but we seldom actively care for it. For example, it is a seemingly small act, but really a huge leap, to reach down during a hike and pick up a piece of litter. Most hikers might leave it to someone else to clean up or rationalize that it wasn't their litter, and walk on. Most might even pass an injured bird and talk themselves into doing nothing because they don't want to spoil their carefully laid plans for the day. I know about these thoughts because I have them myself from time to time: "Oh, why did I have to find this bird when I have to get home to watch 'fill-in-the-blank' tonight?"

But if we are to acknowledge wild places as soul homes, we must take on whatever they ask of us, even at the most mistimed of times. A soul home sometimes has hard edges and thorns that prick us and demand our attention when our minds are protesting, "I'd rather not right now." The soul home's timetable often exasperates the mind's schedule.

This may be why remote trails are seldom flooded with people. Even on the busiest of holiday weekends, I know I will find some solitude on Sky Trail. Most people are in town at the shops, or lounging on the beaches, or lined up in their cars at a fabulous view by the ocean. The trail requires more intimacy, and, with that intimacy, care. It engages all the senses. It ratchets up our awareness of our needs and its own. A soul trail is an immediate family member.

Once we adopt, or are adopted by, a soul trail, our next steps— toward a soul park, town, city, bioregion, country, continent, planet, solar system, and universe—become easier and more familiar. We begin to see ourselves extending our caring and loving energy. When we "realize" everything we see, in the way that Sasaki Roshi wanted me to "realize" that single flower, we begin to feel more deeply at home wherever we are. And then, as most of us do with our living spaces, we keep them clean. We make them welcoming for guests. We make them comfortable and nurturing for ourselves. We make necessary repairs and changes when things break down. Most of all, we treat those spaces with respect, intelligence, and care, honoring their cycles and needs.

Perhaps more importantly, we honor our own cycles and needs, for out of that love and attention comes a heightened awareness of everything that makes up our world. As we begin to identify ourselves as citizens and caretakers of the world, our hopes and prayers for peace, both within ourselves and around us breathe deeper than ever before giving newfound clarity to our purpose. This in turn allows us to re-examine our place in the world so we can help to unravel the tangle of physical, political, religious, and social boundaries that have obstructed and distorted the world for generations. When we allow the grace of connection to take root in our heart, like a delicate, searching, resilient sapling yearning to live, from that moment on, the trail we thought we knew so well suddenly evolves and becomes the Path.

That is my wish for our beautiful blue planet and for all human beings, who influence it most.

Stephen Altschuler is a writer, teacher, and counselor. His other books include *Sacred Paths and Muddy Places: Rediscovering Spirit in Nature* (1993), and *Hidden Walks in the East Bay and Marin: Pathways, Essays, and Yesterdays* (2001). He has also written articles and essays for numerous periodicals.

In addition, he counsels disabled students at Santa Rosa Junior College, and teaches Tai Chi there as well.

Stephen lives with his wife, Ruth, in Sebastopol, California.

At his website, www.mindfulhiker.com, you can learn more about his workshops and talks, based on his books.